W9-BCI-770

RECEIVED
OHIO DOMINICAN
COLLEGE LIBRARY
COLUMBUS, OHIO

OHIO DOMINICAN COLLEGE LIBRARY
COLUMBUS, OHIO 43219

TWAYNE'S WORLD AUTHORS SERIES
A Survey of the World's Literature

JAPAN

Roy B. Teele, University of Texas, Austin

EDITOR

Ishikawa Takuboku

TWAS 539

Ishikawa Takuboku

ISHIKAWA TAKUBOKU

By YUKIHITO HIJIYA

Shikoku Christian College

TWAYNE PUBLISHERS
A DIVISION OF G. K. HALL & CO., BOSTON

Copyright © 1979 by G. K. Hall & Co.

Published in 1979 by Twayne Publishers,
A Division of G. K. Hall & Co.
All Rights Reserved

Printed on permanent/durable acid-free paper and bound
in the United States of America

First Printing

895.61
I79 H
1979

Library of Congress Cataloging in Publication Data

Hijiya, Yukihito.
Ishikawa Takuboku.

(Twayne's world authors series ; TWAS 539 : Japan)
Bibliography: p. 195–99
Includes index.
1. Ishikawa, Takuboku, 1886–1912.   2. Authors,
Japanese—20th century—Biography.   I. Title.
PL809.S5Z656   895.6'1'4   [B]   78-27748
ISBN 0-8057-6381-3

To Robert and Opal Carswell,
my foster parents and dear friends

107920

Contents

About the author

Yukihito Hijiya is Professor of English Literature at Shikoku Christian College, Zentsuji, Kagawa, Japan. He has also taught at Boise State University. After receiving his B.A. in English Literature at Shikoku Christian College he continued his studies at Davidson College. He received an M.A. at Wake Forest University and a Ph.D. at the University of New Mexico. His publications include haiku in English and articles on Byron and Dazai both in English and Japanese.

Preface

This brief study of Ishikawa Takuboku attempts to accomplish two things: first, to give a survey of his life and writing; second, to define his place in the history of modern Japanese literature. In his short life Takuboku tried his hand at every genre except drama and left us essays, novels, poems in the western style and a great number of tanka, a traditional Japanese syllabic verse form in a 5-7-5-7-7 pattern. It is true that some of Takuboku's works, particularly certain of his novels and western style poems, have little literary value. In order to obtain an overall view of the writer, however, and to trace his development it is necessary to consider these less successful works as well as those on which his fame rests. In addition to his literary productions Takuboku regularly kept a diary, which is extremely valuable for an examination of him as a writer and as a thinker. Although there is here no separate chapter specifically devoted to it, the diary is referred to whenever applicable.

Takuboku was first and foremost a tanka poet who derived the subject matter of his poetry from his personal daily experiences. The first chapter, then, is a record of the poet's life, including an examination of his relationship with various literary movements. Chapter 2 deals with Takuboku's essays, which reveal him as a thinker and a critic of Japanese society and literature. Chapter 3 presents Takuboku's attempts to establish himself as a poet in the western poetic form. In the fourth chapter we take a look at Takuboku as a novelist. Chapter 5 treats Takuboku as a tanka poet who displays his full literary power in this form. A thematic and stylistic analysis of representative tanka is undertaken in this chapter, along with an attempt to show that all of Takuboku's literary efforts contributed to his accomplishment as a tanka poet. While Takuboku's essays are a record of his development as a man of letters and reveal the intellectual and literary milieu of his day, it is through his tanka that he established his place in the history of modern Japanese literature. The tanka also comprise the major part of Takuboku's work, and accordingly have received the most attention. The book ends with an evaluation of Takuboku's influence on the modern Japanese tanka. Since each chapter except Chapter 5 separately examines

Takuboku's growth in a particular genre the reader should after the biographical sketch in the first chapter be able to continue without difficulty to read any subsequent chapter.

Translations of some of Takuboku's tanka have been made by several people, whose works are listed in the bibliography. Of these translations those of Carl Sesar are outstanding. His sensitive rendition conveys vividly the feeling of Takuboku's tanka. It is indeed fortunate for us to have such a gifted translator of such delicately and subtly composed tanka as Takuboku's. Of his prose works *The Rōmaji Diary* has been put into English by Donald Keene. For the sake of stylistic uniformity, however, I have translated all quotations from Takuboku myself. Throughout this book Japanese names are cited in the customary order, the family name before the given name or pen name.

In writing this book I am indebted to a great number of Takuboku scholars and critics. There is virtually no page which does not owe something to their contributions. Among the works listed in the Selected Bibliography, I have found the studies by Kunisaki Mokutarō, Odagiri Hideo, Iwaki Yukinori and Imai Yasuko most helpful. I would like to thank the staff of the Japanese National Diet Library for their assistance in locating materials. I am grateful also to Professor Roy E. Teele for his patience in editing my manuscript.

YUKIHITO HIJIYA

Shikoku Christian College
Zentsuji, Kagawa
Japan

Acknowledgments

I should like to express to the following my deep appreciation for permission to quote copyrighted material:

For permission to cite passages from Takuboku's works I am indebted to Ishikawa Reiji and to Chikuma Shobō, Tokyo, publishers of Takuboku's complete works; to Toki Aika for tanka from *Tasogare ni (At Twilight)* and *Fuhei naku (Without Complaints)*; to Saitō Teruko and Iwanami Shoten, Tokyo, publishers, for tanka from *Shakkō (Red Light)* by Saitō Mokichi; to Watanabe Susumu for tanka from *Binbō no Uta (Songs of Privation)* by Watanabe Junzō; to Nishimura Kaho for tanka from *Toshi Kyojūsha (City Dwellers)* and *Gairoju (Trees Along a Street)* by Nishimura Yōkichi; to Yasunari Motosaburō for tanka from *Binbō to Koi (Poverty and Love)* and *Chūōkōron* (June, 1923) by Yasunari Jirō; to Susukida Katsura for "Hagame no Uta" ("To a Broken Pot") from *Yuku Haru (The Passing Spring)* by Susukida Kyūkin.

Chronology

1886 February 20, Ishikawa Hajime born at Hinoto Village, Iwate Prefecture.

1887 Ishikawa family moved to Shibutami Village near Hinoto.

1898 Completed studies at Shibutami Elementary School and passed the entrance examination to Morioka Middle School at the capital of the prefecture.

1899 Became acquainted with Horiai Setsuko. Began to show interest in literature.

1900 April, the third year at Morioka Middle School. Interest in literature grew. Introduced to Kindaichi Kyōsuke, later a well known philologist, famous for his studies in the Ainu language and literature.

1902 January 11 and 12, criticism of *Young Leaves of Grass* by Kanbara Ariake published in the *Iwate Daily News*. April, moved up to the fifth year of the middle school. July, cheated during the midterm examination. After summer vacation decided against returning to school. In the meantime his tanka was published in *Morning Star*, a noted literary magazine of the day. October 31, went to Tokyo. Met Yosano Tekkan, poet and editor of *Morning Star*, and his wife. Soon fell ill.

1903 February 27, accompanied by father returned to Shibutami. May, published "The Ideas of Richard Wagner" in the *Iwate Daily News*. Early November, encouraged by Tekkan started writing poems in the western style. December, adopted pen name "Takuboku."

1904 January, engaged to Setsuko. October, made a second trip to Tokyo in the hope of having western style poems published in book form.

1905 May 3, *Longing* published. May 30, married Setsuko. September, edited and published *A Little World*, a literary magazine.

1906 April, took a position as a part time teacher at Shibutami Elementary School. June, went to Tokyo again; came home with enthusiasm for the Naturalistic movement. July, began to write *Clouds Are Geniuses,* which he revised in November. Began *The Funeral Procession* in November also. December 29, daughter Kyōko born. From November 23 to December 3, wrote "A Letter from the Forest."

1907   March, "A Letter from the Forest" published. April, dismissed from Shibutami Elementary School for inciting pupils' strike against the principal. May, moved to Hakodate in Hokkaido alone to become editor of *Crimson Medic,* a local literary magazine. Soon became friends with Miyazaki Daishirō. June, employed as a part time teacher at a municipal elementary school in Hakodate. Made acquaintance of Tachibana Chieko, a fellow teacher. July, family joined him. September, left Hakodate to assume a newspaper job in Sapporo. Two weeks later resigned to work as a reporter in Otaru. Resigned in December.

1908   January, took job as editor of a local newspaper in Kushiro. February, wrote "One Branch on a Table" for the *Kushiro News.* Became acquainted with geisha Koyakko. April 24, made the last journey to Tokyo. May, completed *The Hospital Window.* June 23, sudden overflow of tanka, which lasted two days. November, *The Shadow of a Bird* serialized in the *Mainichi* newspaper until the end of the year.

1909   March, took a position as proofreader for the *Asahi* newspaper. From April 7 to June 1 kept *The Rōmaji Diary.* From November 30 to December 7, published "From Yumi-chō: Poems to Eat" in the *Mainichi,* and in the December issue of *The Pleiades,* a literary magazine, had "Sporadic Feelings and Reflections" published. Also in December, a series of poems under the title "A Study of the Heart" published in the *Mainichi* newspaper.

1910   June 6, with the arrest of Kōtoku Shūsui the High Treason Incident broke out. From the end of May to the middle of June, produced *Our Gang and He.* August, wrote "The Present State of the Age of Repression," which was published posthumously. October 4, son born but lived only three weeks. December 1, *A Handful of Sand* published.

1911   January 13, met Toki Aika and with him planned to publish a magazine, *Tree and Fruit.* Around January 23, began to compose tanka which were to be included in *Sad Toys.* February 1, hospitalized for peritonitis. March, discharged from the hospital. From June 15 to 17, composed a series of poems under the title "After Endless Discussions," which were later compiled in *Power and Poetry*. August, rented a house.

1912   March 7, mother died of tuberculosis. April 13, Takuboku died of tuberculosis. June 20, *Sad Toys* published.

CHAPTER 1

The Making of a Poet

ISHIKAWA Takuboku was born Ishikawa Hajime on February 20, 1886, at Hinoto Village, Iwate Prefecture, in the northern part of Honshū. His father, Ittei, was a Zen priest, and Takuboku, the third of four children, was the only son of the family. When Takuboku was two years old, Ittei was appointed to the priesthood of Hōtoku Temple of Shibutami Village, not far from Takuboku's birthplace, and the family moved there. Shibutami, then, became the home about which Takuboku was later to sing in his tanka and write in his novels.

As the only son of the family, Takuboku was the center of his parents' attention. The household revolved about the young boy. The memoir of his sister, Mitsuko, gives a good illustration of the parents' indulgence of the boy:

My brother's self-indulgence was such that his stubborn asking for a piece of *yubeshi* bean-jam-bun used to wake everybody up even at midnight. Mother would often give in to his pleas and get up to make one for him. No matter how cold the day was or no matter how late it was, this was the typical scene. . . . Not only did he manipulate Mother's love as he wished in this manner but also he enjoyed Father's; whenever Father made a tool, he used to pronounce it to be Hajime's and wrote himself "Ishikawa Hajime's possession" on it.[1]

As a result, Takuboku developed a consciousness of being special and a strong individualistic personality, bordering on arrogance. This trait was intensified when upon finishing at the top of the class in elementary school he was labeled a child prodigy.

Takuboku's entering Morioka Middle School in Morioka, the capital of Iwate Prefecture, laid the ground for his future. It was the spring of 1898 and Takuboku was twelve years old. He immediately

17

made himself known among a group of students who enjoyed writing tanka. Among them was Kindaichi Kyōsuke, two years senior, who was to remain one of his two closest friends.[2] Kindaichi had already had several tanka published in *Myōjō (Morning Star)*, a prestigious literary magazine of the day. The magazine was edited and published by Yosano Tekkan, who was also head of the group called, after the title of the magazine, the Myōjō school of poetry. Kindaichi was already a member of the group when Takuboku came to know him. Borrowing a copy of the magazine from Kindaichi, Takuboku immediately began studying the characteristics of the school, which had a decided romantic tone, and submitted tanka written in a similar vein. His first published tanka, in the October, 1902, issue of *Morning Star* was "chi ni someshi uta o wagayo no nagori nite sasurai koko ni no ni sakebu aki "Leaving a blood-stained poem as a memento of my life, I wander here—autumn in the bleak wilderness." For a sixteen-year-old country middle school student to have a poem published in Tokyo in a toprated literary magazine was a remarkable achievement indeed. While writing tanka for *Morning Star* as well as for the school literary magazine, *The Benign Divine Spirit* of which he was editor, the young Takuboku also wrote articles and book reviews, such as a critique of a collection of poems by Kanbara Ariake, *Young Leaves of Grass*, written for the local newspaper, the *Iwate Daily News*.

Another significant event during Takuboku's middle school days in Morioka was his encounter with Horiai Setsuko, whom he met during his first year there. The Horiai family were neighbors of Takuboku's sister, Sada, and her husband Tamura Suekichi, with whom Takuboku lived from 1899 to 1902. His acquaintance with Setsuko blossomed into romance leading to marriage and family responsibilities for Takuboku at an early age. The destiny of Takuboku as a writer and as a man was thus determined in his middle school days.

On October 31, 1902, Takuboku left Morioka Middle School for good and journeyed to Tokyo alone. The reason for his sudden departure half-way through his last year of school was recently made clear by Yuza Shōgo. Takuboku's increasing interest in literature and his relationship with Setsuko seem to have deprived him of his interest in other fields of study. Because of lack of preparation he had asked an honor student to help him with the final examination in mathematics. Both Takuboku and the other student were caught and suspended from school; Takuboku regretted very much having involved one of the top students in his misdemeanor. He decided not to return to school and left for Tokyo.[3] Leaving Morioka Middle School marked the end of his formal education, which in turn meant the gate was closed for any future career of social prominence and financial security. Perhaps without being fully aware of what he was doing, he rushed headlong into a situation that would lead to eventual poverty and frustration.

Two plans were in Takuboku's mind when he came to Tokyo: one was to attempt transfer to a middle school in Tokyo. He soon found that there was no way to enter any school in the middle of the school year, and thus his first plan was unrealized. The second purpose in coming to Tokyo, to affiliate himself with the Myōjō poets, succeeded. In November he attended a gathering of the poets of the "new style poetry" movement, which included Yosano Tekkan, his wife, Akiko, Kanbara Ariake, Susukida Kyūkin, Hirade Shū and others.

The movement had been introduced by the publication of *A Selection of Poems in the New Style* in 1882, of which Donald Keene provides a good summary: "It included fourteen translations of English and American poems, one French poem translated from an English version, and five original poems by the compilers. Among the English poems were 'The Charge of the Light Brigade,' 'Elegy Written in a Country Churchyard,' the 'To be or not to be' soliloquy, and two translations of Longfellow's 'A Psalm of Life'."[4] With form, style and content completely different from those of traditional haiku and waka or Chinese poetry, which had long been the definition of "poem," these translations of western poems indeed marked the beginning of modern Japanese poetry. The book's great impact on the Japanese literary world of that day was due more to the fact that it set forth new possibilities of subject matter, length and forms of poems and freedom of language than to the gracefulness of the translations; the Japanese renditions, in fact, were far from graceful. While it is true that liberated from the conventional conception of poetry, some aspiring poets went so far as to believe that any subject was acceptable for poetry or that any language could be poetic, it is also true that others were awakened to the fact that poetry had far more possibilities than had previously been imagined. Thus, as Keene points out, the term "poems in the new style" (*"shintai-shi"*) of the title "came to be employed as the normal designation of the new poetry."[5] Modern Japanese poetry in the new style attained maturity with the publication of Shimazaki Tōson's *Seedlings* in 1897, which captivated the imagination of the readers.

At the time when Takuboku came to Tokyo the "poetry in the new style" movement was already far advanced. Among the poets who distinguished themselves in this movement were Susukida Kyūkin and Kanbara Ariake, whose names were well known among literary circles when Takuboku became a member of the Myōjō group. Though he had not yet tried writing a poem in the new style, he must surely have been stimulated by the rich literary environment of outstanding poets enthusiastic over the new poetry.

Takuboku's stay in Tokyo was cut short, however, because of illness, which made it necessary for him to leave the center of literary activity. Tekkan, just before Takuboku left for Shibutami, wisely advised him to write poems in the new style rather than tanka. Tekkan saw no originality in Takuboku's tanka, the style of which had been merely an imitation of Akiko's. Takuboku readily followed this advice and sent five poems to Tekkan, who noticed at once, though the poems betrayed a debt to Ariake and Kyūkin, that Takuboku possessed extraordinary talent. It is said that it was at this time that Tekkan gave to seventeen-year-old Ishikawa Hajime the pen name "Takuboku" ("Woodpecker"), taken from the title of one of the poems published in *Morning Star,* "The Woodpecker's Song."

During 1903 and 1904 as Takuboku continued to publish his poems in *Morning Star* and other literary magazines as well, the public began to recognize him as a young poet of genius. Thus his future began to seem bright: his reputation was established and he was engaged to Setsuko. In October, 1904, encouraged by his success, he again went to Tokyo, this time hoping to get his poems published in book form. A collection of his poems under the title *Longing* was published in Tokyo the following year, the year Takuboku was married. At the age of twenty, just when life seemed to be so full of promise for him, Takuboku's real troubles began. No sooner was he married than he was confronted with serious financial problems: responsibility not only for himself and Setsuko but also for his parents. Takuboku's father had neglected to pay the duties of the temple to the regional headquarters; some of the fees had been used, without Takuboku's knowing, for the latter's trip to Tokyo in

October of 1904. Ittei was therefore divested of the office of resident priest of Hōtoku Temple, and the family's source of income was gone. Takuboku had thought that the income from the newly published collection of poems would enable him to support his household, but *Longing* brought virtually no remuneration for him. He therefore submitted articles to the *Iwate Daily News* for a meager compensation. Further, in the hope of gaining additional income, Takuboku published *A Little World*, a magazine which included not only a poem of his own but also articles by such prestigious literary figures of the day as Iwano Hōmei, Masamune Hakuchō, Tsunajima Ryōsen, Osanai Kaoru and Yosano Tekkan. The publication failed, however, to produce enough capital for a second issue.

In January, 1906, Ittei left the household in the hope that his absence would ease the burden imposed on his son. He went to Nobechi, in neighboring Aomori Prefecture, to be cared for in the household of his brother-in-law, also a priest. In March, through the influence of Setsuko's father, Takuboku was given a position as a part time teacher at Shibutami Elementary School, which he had attended in his childhood. In his diary Takuboku recorded his great delight in the appointment:

I have bid adieu to the nine months' life in Morioka, and my new life at my home town Shibutami has begun today [March 4, 1906]. . . . Why have I chosen this far away place for my new life? That question can be answered simply: Shibutami is my home, the native place that has the closest relation to me of all other places on this earth. The incomparably sweet magic power inherent in the word, "home village," has been for a long time drawing the magnet of my heart deeply and forcibly. Love, poetry, anguish, pride, tears and home—these have been everything of my inner life up until the present time. Some people say that wherever one goes, there are green mountains, and that a youth of the spirit should not be attached only to the small world of "home," . . . but "home" to me is, as it were, the natural palace built for me by the special grace of a god.[6]

Despite the low salary he would receive, Takuboku was exultant at the prospect of returning to his old home.

In April, since there was still a slim chance that Ittei might be restored to his former position, Takuboku called his father back to Shibutami. Ittei stayed there for a year, hoping for reappointment.

During a brief break in June, Takuboku went to Tokyo to appeal to
have his father reinstated, but in vain: in December of that year
another priest was to come to Hōtoku Temple, and thus it was
almost certain that Ittei would be deprived of the position completely. For Takuboku himself, however, the third visit to Tokyo
was a fruitful one. On this visit he was introduced to Naturalism,
then a strong new literary movement, and particularly to the novel,
which had begun to flourish with the rapid spread of the movement.[7] While he intuitively sensed the significance of the movement making such a great impact upon literary circles in Tokyo, it
should be noted that Takuboku's interest lay not so much in the
movement itself as in experimenting with the novel. His sen-
sibilities at this point were too closely attuned to Romanticism for
him to embrace Naturalism wholeheartedly. On his return from
Tokyo Takuboku set his hand to his first novel, *Clouds Are
Geniuses*. By the end of the year he had written two more novels,
Vestige and *The Funeral Procession*, which was published in the
December issue of *Morning Star*.

Takuboku was in charge of second graders, but as an extracurricular activity he also taught English to older pupils. During his
one year of teaching at Shibutami, he was the most popular teacher
at the school. From his experience there, Takuboku got the material
for his first novel, *Clouds Are Geniuses*.

The birth of a daughter in December brought so much joy to the
heart of the young father as to make the pecuniary hardships seem
insignificant: "I am surely excited, content and happy. At the end of
my eighteenth year I was recognized by a literary circle as a new
poet, at twenty I had a first collection of poetry published and in the
same year I was married to Setsuko. And now at twenty-one, I not
only have begun to write novels but also have become a father all of
a sudden. . . . I am not sad; no, no reason to be sad" (V, 115). But the
truth of the matter was that Kyōko's birth meant an additional financial burden for the family. In March, 1907, unable to cope with the
pressure imposed by the villagers who were opposed to his return to
the temple and pained at seeing the wretched condition of his son's
life, Ittei once more left Shibutami, never to return to the village
again.

His father's leaving did nothing to ease Takuboku's financial burden; Ittei's departure only brought into clearer focus the problems
the whole family had been facing. Takuboku determined to find

employment which would provide him with a better income, and through the assistance of a friend, Matsuoka Rodō, made arrangements to go to Hokkaido. In April he submitted a letter of resignation, but before the request had been taken up by the school officials, Takuboku instigated a student strike against the principal, whom he disliked. As a result, the principal, victim though he was, was blamed for the strike, and transferred to another post while Takuboku was dismissed from the school with no other alternative than to leave the village. The animosity of certain of the villagers toward the Ishikawas, aroused by Ittei's persistent attempts to return to their temple, was further intensified by Takuboku's drastic act. The mixed feelings with which he left the village Takuboku expressed later in a tanka:

ishi o mote owaruru gotoku	as if driven out by stoning
furusato o ideshi kanashimi	I left the village
kiyuru toki nashi	that sorrow never fades away

Takuboku thus departed from Shibutami never to set foot in the beloved village again, and began the uncertain life of a wanderer.

I A Year of Wandering

Leaving his wife and daughter with his wife's family and his mother with a friend's, Takuboku in May, 1907, left for a new life in Hokkaido. His friend, Matsuoka Rodō, was a member of the literary group called Circle of Medics in the port city of Hakodate. The group had been organized in the fall of the preceding year by four young men, Namiki Takeo, Iwasaki Tadashi, Yoshino Shōzō and Matsuoka Seinosuke (Rodō). Three of Takuboku's poems, "The Ginko Tree," "The Wild Goose" and "The Snowy Evening," had been published in the first issue of their magazine, *Crimson Medic.* Thus Takuboku's name was already well known to them. He happened to write to Matsuoka just at the time when the group was searching for a new editor who could devote full time to the magazine. Takuboku was immediately offered the position.

This new circle of friends was a group of energetic young people of sensibility who often gathered and composed tanka together. Takuboku's interest in writing tanka was revived by the lively atmosphere of the group. He developed a close friendship with

Miyazaki Daishirō, whose pen name was Ikuu. Ikuu, the son of a wealthy bean paste manufacturer, was the financier of the magazine. It is hardly an exaggeration to say that from this time on Takuboku and his family lived on the generosity of Miyazaki until the friendship grew sour four years later.

In the meantime Takuboku obtained a position as a part time teacher at an elementary school in Hakodate. It was there that he became acquainted with Tachibana Chieko, a fellow teacher about whom he sang in twenty-two tanka included in *A Handful of Sand*. The position provided Takuboku with a regular income, meager though it was. This enabled him to call Setsuko and Kyōko to join him in July, and his mother in August. In August he was also invited to join the staff of The *Hakodate Daily News*. While working as a reporter he began a poetry section in the paper and was given the responsibility of selecting poems for publication. In addition, he wrote essays for the paper concerning social and political problems; thus the *Hakodate Daily News* benefited from his diverse literary talents.

Now, once more, just when the young man's future and the family livelihood seemed secured, fate turned against him. On August 25 a huge fire broke out in Hakodate and the headquarters of *Crimson Medic*, the *Hakodate Daily News* building and the elementary school, all were burnt to ashes. Circle of Medics could not resume publication of their magazine, for Miyazaki, in military training at that time, was far away from Hakodate; unable to secure financial resources, the group decided to dissolve. Takuboku was out of a job again.

Through the recommendation of Mukai Eitarō, a member of Circle of Medics who worked at the Forestry Department at the Hokkaido Prefectural Office, Takuboku soon gained employment with the *North Gate Newspaper* as a proofreader. Leaving his family again in Hakodate, Takuboku left for Sapporo. He later wrote a tanka recalling that day:

ame tsuyoku furu yo no kisha no   night rain—
taema naku shizuku nagaruru   running endlessly
mado garasu kana   down the window of the train

No sooner had he begun his new job as proofreader than he was offered a different position, this time at the *Otaru Daily*, a newspaper just being established. So Takuboku left Sapporo after only two weeks' stay; but the city of Sapporo, as described in the opening of his novel of the same name, remained always beautiful in his memory:

> Since I have lived about half of my life as a wanderer, I reminisce of many places with nostalgia. Of these, no other place has left in my heart such a fond, though rushed, memory as Sapporo from my two weeks' stay there. The scene of the capital in the middle of the Ishikari plain—a large country town with wide streets, quiet with many trees, with western style houses forming a line dispersedly, and each large building appearing to be pressed against the boundless sky—often returns to my mind and attracts me like the kindness of an aunt or something. (III, 187)

At Otaru Takuboku worked with Noguchi Ujō, himself a poet. He continued to write essays, poems and book reviews, and his virtuosity as a writer was immediately recognized by the editor-in-chief of the company. Because of internal struggles among members of the staff, however, Takuboku soon left the newspaper, once more plunging himself and his family into poverty. They entered the New Year of 1908 without a penny.

Pecuniary difficulties, however, did not prevent Takuboku from keeping himself well informed on current trends in Japanese society. In fact, these very hardships may have intensified his awareness of social problems. On January 4 he went to listen to a public lecture by socialist Nishikawa Mitsujirō and recorded his impression:

> In essence, socialism occupies one small corner of my so-called long-term liberation movement. Socialism is not only a warming-up exercise before we achieve the final great emancipation but an urgent matter that has appeared suddenly before us. This movement, inheriting various freedom movements from the former generation attempts to set the laborers, the people ranking the lowest in social class, free from the capitalists so as to give them most essential freedom. Its theoretical position has been today thoroughly examined, and in spite of various persecutions, it has infiltrated deep into the heart of all people. The period of studying socialism is already past, and it is high time for one to investigate the ways and means to realize the philosophy of the movement.
>
> Further, this movement is not merely for freeing oppressed workers from capitalists; it ought to take as its ideal the liberation of all people from unjust suffering in life. It was a pity to see that the thinking of the people present at the gathering today did not reach that far. (V, 193–94)

A youthful, idealistic observation and analysis of socialism, the passage reveals not only his sensitivity to world events but also his keen insight into the essential nature of the movement. Takuboku was interested in socialism at this point in his career not so much because of its promise of a better future but because it reflected his own view of life formed naturally by his actual experience of hardship. Financial limitations, however, kept him from actual participation in the movement; and when Takuboku moved to Kushiro, his last place of residence in Hokkaido, he put socialism out of his mind completely until 1910.

His next position was at the *Kushiro News*, the owner of which was also the president of the *Otaru Daily* for which Takuboku had previously worked. Takuboku was nominally appointed to the post of editor of the third page, the section dealing with social events, but in actual practice he was editor of the entire paper. He made a number of innovations in the paper, adding such new sections as a poetry column and a regular account of events in the world of the geisha, a section to which he himself contributed. The chief source of his information was Koyakko, a geisha of whom he was particularly fond and about whom he later composed several tanka, published in *Sad Toys*. This unusual coverage had great appeal for the readers, making it possible for the paper to outstrip its rival in content as well as circulation. Takuboku's other writings during those days include "One Branch on a Table," an essay about the Naturalistic movement, and other essays concerning socio-political issues, Takuboku by and large enjoyed his busy life in Kushiro, though it was not without frustration. In his diary he wrote: "Forty days have already passed since I came to Kushiro. While I have been devoting my time and energy for the newspaper, I have not picked up a book even once" (V, 223).

The newspaper work into which the search for financial security had led him, though in retrospect proving worthwhile for his later writings, did not satisfy his sense of vocation. His calling was to be a writer, and he could not settle for less: "Ah, I have made a mistake! My calling is, after all, for literature. What am I confused about? What am I worried about? If there were a way to get food, I should be devoting myself only to literary activities without worrying. Without literature, there is no meaning for my existence, nor purpose, nor aspiration" (V, 166). This desire for an opportunity to devote his energy to writing was expressed again in "From Yumi-chō," an essay written in Tokyo the following year. His excitement over the Naturalistic movement and frustration at being away from the center of literary activity are vividly described in the essay:

When I was running toward the far north in search of food, the echo of the famous new movement that had brought about the unity of literature with thought reached me also. My resentment of fantasy literature [Romantic literature], combined with a little experience I had gained from my actual life, eventually led me to accept the spirit of the new movement. Taking a glance at it from afar, I felt as if I was witnessing at the top of a dark mountain a house from which I had just escaped catching fire and going up in flame instantly. Even now when I think about it, I cannot forget the feeling I had then. (IV, 209–10)

By the time one year had passed, his mind was made up: "It was the conclusion arrived at after a year of wandering that I go back to Tokyo again to try my literary destiny" (V, 249).

II *Tokyo Again*

Entrusting his family to the care of the Miyazakis in Hakodate, Takuboku, now twenty-two years old, sailed to Tokyo in April, 1908. Thanks to Miyazaki's selfless generosity, the family deprived of the breadwinner did not starve; but one can imagine how difficult must have been the life of separation from their loved one. Takuboku had misgivings about leaving them behind, yet he could not sacrifice his aspirations; he sacrificed his family instead. In Tokyo he found lodging at Seki-shin-kan, where his old friend Kindaichi Kyōsuke had been staying, and once more made contact with literary circles. To begin with he and Yosano Tekkan attended a tanka composition gathering at the house of Mori Ōgai, one of the most celebrated writers of the Meiji era, a gathering which included also such poets as Itō Sachio, Sasaki Nobutsuna, Kitahara Hakushū and Saitō Mokichi.

Takuboku's major interest at this time lay, however, not in tanka but in the novel. He was expecting, moreover, that the publication of his novels would provide him with a livelihood. He applied himself with energy to his self-appointed task and within one month had produced "Mr. Kikuchi," *The Hospital Window*, "Mother," "Velvet" and "Two Streams of Blood," all together 300 pages in the standard text. Overconfident perhaps because of his early successes in Tokyo and Hokkaido, Takuboku naively assumed that his novels would be readily accepted by publishers. But even the influence of Kindaichi and Mori was of no avail; Takuboku's writings were repeatedly turned down. Now his frustration and disillusionment were compounded. With no means of livelihood, it was impossible to bring his family to Tokyo as he had intended; and even worse for the writer, he began to have doubts about his capability as a novelist.

On the evening of June 23, two months after coming to Tokyo, in the midst of disillusionment and frustration, Takuboku began to write tanka. Once he had started, poem after poem flowed from his pen, and he composed successively fifty-five tanka. He wrote fifty more on the following day and 141 the day after that. Takuboku himself was surprised at this sudden outpouring: "All my head has become tanka. Whatever I see or hear, all turns into a tanka. From this afternoon to two o'clock in the morning I composed 141. Nearly forty of them are about my parents, and I wrote them in tears" (V, 283). From this abundance he selected 114 tanka for publication in the July issue of *Morning Star*. Although he had temporarily reached a dead end in writing novels, he had in composing tanka found an outlet for his frustration. It was his tanka, composed in his own unique style, that determined the place Takuboku holds in the history of modern Japanese tanka. Two collections of his tanka were published in 1910 and 1912 under the titles *A Handful of Sand* and *Sad Toys*.

Writing tanka granted Takuboku some measure of relief from the wretchedness of his daily existence, but only temporarily. With no financial resources of his own he continued to live on the mercy and generosity of his friends; in particular Kindaichi in Tokyo and Miyazaki in Hakodate were friends in the truest sense of the word. Miyazaki sent money whenever it was asked for, and Kindaichi, though far less prosperous, gave Takuboku what financial assistance he could, even going so far as to sell some of his books in order to pay room rent for his friend. The more Takuboku received from the hands of these friends, however, the more this dependence became a reminder of his own failure as a provider for himself and his family:

When I woke up I found it had been raining heavily. As I was thinking on my pillow half-asleep, I came to want to die. I am afraid that only in death can one seek peace of mind. The anguish of life! If I was alone, the problem would be a little better, but I well know that my old father is living a life of a hanger-on in the countryside far away, my old mother, wife, daughter and sister are taken care of by my friend! Ah, what should I do? This month, I cannot pay the room rent again.

"To be, or not to be?"

I want to die, but I do not try to die. What a sad thing, I cannot govern myself at will. (V, 285)

Takuboku's diary of June and July of 1908 reveals his emotional distress and his preoccupation with suicide: "By streetcar I came as far as Kasuga-chō; then when I walked up the wide hill, I got sweaty again. A streetcar came down the hill rapidly. Suddenly, I wanted to jump in front of it, but I restrained myself with the thought: I am carrying a fan on which a tanka of mine is written; if I commit suicide, people will immediately know who I am. So I did not kill myself" (V, 307). Takuboku's despair was finally softened a little in November when his novel *The Shadow of a Bird* was serialized in the Tokyo *Mainichi* newspaper.

Even in his depression Takuboku kept in contact with the group advocating the new style poetry. Publication of *Morning Star* ended with the 100th issue in November, 1908, and Takuboku began to work with Hirano Mari and other members of the group to publish a different magazine. The new magazine, *The Pleiades*, was projected to represent the younger generation of the Myōjō school, but Takuboku broke with the group after the publication of the second issue. His view of tanka was opposed to that of Hirano and others, which tended to stress the aesthetic view of poetry. Takuboku's experience had led him to the conviction that art for art's sake is of no value.

In March, 1909, Takuboku was given a position as proofreader for the Tokyo *Asahi* newspaper. Through he now had employment that guaranteed a regular income, he was reluctant to send for his family. In *The Rōmaji Diary* is recorded an account of the inner conflict he was experiencing at this time. He was simply not ready to curb his personal freedom and assume responsibility for others. But his sense of moral obligation finally won out. Setsuko, Kyōko and his mother came to Tokyo in June, and together they made a new home in a rented room over a barber shop.

Their life in Tokyo, however, was not a happy one. Because of large accumulated debts, the income Takuboku received from his new work was far from adequate for the support of four people, and the financial burden was increased when Setsuko developed pleuritis. Cheerful dispositions might have enabled the family to surmount their difficulties, but there was constant bickering between mother-in-law and daughter-in-law, both of them wearied and irritable because of their many privations. One of Takuboku's tanka presents a graphic picture of the situation:

neko o kawaba,	decided to keep a cat
sono neko ga mata arasoi no	only to quarrel over it.
tane to naruramu,	my cheerless household.
kanashiki waga ya.	

In October Setsuko suddenly returned to her home in Morioka taking three-year-old Kyōko with her.

Setsuko gave as her reasons for leaving a desire to return to the country to cure her illness and also to help her sister prepare for her coming marriage to Miyazaki Ikuu. Takuboku knew very well, however, that the true reason for her leaving was that life in Tokyo had become intolerable for her: the life of poverty combined with Takuboku's lack of concern for the family's welfare prompted Setsuko's radical action. Her departure was a big blow to him, and though she returned after two weeks, the incident marked a significant turning point for Takuboku. Five months later he wrote to Miyazaki concerning the whole matter:

Ever since the shock I received at the end of last fall, my thinking has been drastically changed. I seem not to be the same person that I used to be in every nook and corner of my heart; I had almost become a student of the most certainly practical philosophy. The unity and completeness of both physical and mental life—this used to be my motto, for which I strove and worked very diligently. Finally today I have discovered that in our present life, an attempt at the completeness of life consequentially leads itself, contrary to our expectations, to destruction. (VII, 296)

Takuboku's works, particularly the essays, written between Setsuko's departure and the letter to Miyazaki reveal a marked change in his attitudes toward his life and work. He had come to Tokyo in order to find self-fulfillment through writing, but his life there had not been at all what he had anticipated. He had in short been naive about himself and about life. The irksome details of everyday life which demanded his attention slowly awakened him to perceive things around him in broader perspective and led him to form a different view of the relationship between literature and life, between a writer as an individual and his daily existence. This growth in his perception is most apparent in the two important essays written in November and December: "From Yumi-chō: Poems to Eat," a summary of Takuboku's view of poetry and the poet and the current literary movement of Naturalism, and "Sporadic Feelings and Reflections." In these essays Takuboku's theory of literature and its relationship to life is succinctly presented, a view characterized by his criticism of Naturalism.

The following year, 1910, marked a significant turning point in Takuboku's political philosophy. In May it was announced that the police had uncovered an anarchist plot to assassinate the emperor, and in the following month Kōtoku Shūsui, the alleged leader of the group, and other anarchists and socialists were arrested. Kōtoku was included among the twenty-six persons who were immediately indicted for high treason. This is the case today known as the High Treason Incident or the Kōtoku Incident. The trial, which was under complete control of the prosecution, was conducted in a closed courtroom. All the defense attorneys could do was look over the records submitted by the prosecutors, who in fact did not make at all clear the reasons for the charges brought against Kōtoku. On January 18, 1911, verdict was passed: twenty-four of the twenty-six were sentenced to death. The number of death sentences was lowered to twelve, however, on the following day by an imperial pardon; the twelve who escaped capital punishment were sentenced to life imprisonment. Executions were carried out swiftly: they began with Kōtoku Shūsui on January 24 and ended with Sugano Suga on the following day. The case was closed within eight months after the arrests of the accused.[8]

It has since been proved that of the anarchists apprehended first in May, 1910, Miyashita Takichi and Sugano Suga had plotted to murder the emperor, though they had never reached the point of actually taking steps to carry out their plan, and that Kōtoku Shūsui had had nothing to do with the plot at all. As a matter of fact, the real conspiracy had been on the part of the state, which had plotted to wipe out anarchists and socialists openly opposed to the increasingly imperialistic domestic and foreign policies of the Meiji government. In order to strengthen the power of the autocratic state, the government needed an excuse to silence the opposition and so framed the treason case, using Kōtoku and others as scapegoats. The government conspiracy was successful, for the news of the alleged plot to murder the emperor horrified the public. The government lost no time vigorously expanding suppression, with the result that the socialist movement was thoroughly subdued for the next ten years. Japan thus entered what is now referred to as "the ten years' winter" at the end of the Meiji era.

Takuboku's reaction to these events is of special interest, for as he admitted one year later, the incident had indeed led him finally to accept socialism. In his diary at the end of 1911 he listed the significant events that had taken place during the preceding year. Concerning the High Treason Incident he writes:

June—The conspiracy incident involving Kōtoku Shūsui and others was uncovered, and it brought about a radical change in my views. Little by little, I collected books and magazines on socialism.

This year I have found the key for unifying my personality, taste and inclination: the cause of socialism. Concerning this matter, I have done more thinking and reading and have had more talks than ever. (VI, 225, 226)

His revived interest in socialism led in turn to a renewal of his friendship with Nishikawa Mitsujirō, the public lecturer on socialism whom he had met once in Hokkaido. Takuboku's imagination, inflamed by this incident, gave birth to one of the most significant documents of the Meiji era, "The Present State of the Age of Repression: The Fall of Authoritative Power and of Pure Naturalism and the Examination of Tomorrow," a work that reveals Takuboku's youthful passion for changing the structure of the repressive society of Japan while expressing his clear rejection of the Naturalist movement.

The year 1910 was also a year of a great loss for the Ishikawa family. On October 4 a son was born to Takuboku and Setsuko, but the baby lived only twenty-three days. Placed at the end of A

Handful of Sand are eight tanka which the grieving father composed about the dead child.

III   *Takuboku and Socialism*

The period of Takuboku's serious concern with socialism was short and intense. The High Treason Incident spurred his interest in it, and he applied himself to examining every aspect of the case. One of the defense lawyers, Hirade Shū, a former member of the Myōjō group, happened to be a close friend of Takuboku. From him Takuboku gathered a considerable amount of inside information not only concerning the trial itself but also about the accused, particularly Kōtoku Shūsui. The entries in Takuboku's diary beginning with January 3, 1911, show his continuing interest in the trial. He passed the nights of January 23 and 24 in copying the records of the trial and compiling his document of the Kōtoku Incident. The fruit of this dedicated effort was *Japanese Anarchist Conspiracy Incident: Proceedings and Related Phenomena*, a detailed account of the trial, and *A Letter from Prison* [Takuboku's title], a letter from Kōtoku Shūsui to his lawyers from prison, with notes and commentary by Takuboku. It was not until after World War II that these works were made public.

Now a confirmed socialist, Takuboku was ready to declare his convictions: "I believe that the existing social system must be destroyed. This is not an academic theory of mine but a conclusion derived from my actual life experience of the past few years. Some day I wish to express my belief in action. I have long hesitated to call myself a socialist, but now I do not any longer. . . . I am dissatisfied with all the old thoughts and systems" (VII, 325–26). He had earlier become acquainted with the young poet Toki Aika (1885–   ). Takuboku, attracted by the revolutionary style of Toki's tanka, began to make plans with him for the joint publication of a magazine, hoping thereby to hasten the realization of his political ideals. The purpose of the magazine, to be entitled *Tree and Fruit*, Takuboku described in a letter to Hirade Shū:

The goal of the magazine is to "bring up even a hundred or two hundred young people, who can at once unify their thoughts for the sake of the advancement of the age when we or others in the future present it to them." To the extent that the magazine is not stopped by censorship from being placed on the market and to the degree that it does not disgrace the name of literature, we plan to ask the readers in a passive way to grow aware of the present situation of young people as well as the internal events of national life. And if it is possible after one or two years, we want to see our magazine regarded as the forerunner of *the socialist movement that has appeared in the literary world.* [Stress is Takuboku's] (VII, 332)

This ideal is exactly what he had put forth in "The Present State of the Age of Repression": to lead young people to a critical scrutiny of the present for the sake of a better future and to give active expression to his convictions concerning the value of the freedom of the individual. Despite their enthusiasm, however, the pair were faced from the beginning with formidable obstacles, which eventually forced them to abandon their original plan. Takuboku was hospitalized with chronic peritonitis, leaving to Toki the entire burden of the search for a publisher. Toki, receiving only promises and procrastination, switched from one publisher to another in an effort to put the magazine out on schedule. Money sent by Miyazaki to pay Takuboku's hospital bill was used for the magazine and eventually lost; the publisher, though he had violated the publication agreement, refused to return the money Takuboku had advanced. Defeated, Takuboku stepped down completely from the plan, leaving Toki to handle affairs as best he could. Format and content changed, the magazine in its final form turned out to be an ordinary literary one, far from the original intention.

After about a month in the hospital Takuboku was released in March of 1911. He still required nursing care but continued to write, mostly tanka and poems in the western style. During the month of June he wrote eleven poems which he edited and compiled into one group under the title of *Power and Poetry.* In July Setsuko herself developed catarrhal pneumonia, and the small, inconvenient room over the barber shop had become a room of the sick. In August they decided to rent a house, something all the family had long desired. All the necessary expenses were again taken care of by Miyazaki's ungrudging benevolence. But the inhabitants of the house were all in poor health, and Takuboku had no leisure to savor the pleasures of living in a place of his own: "My house is a house of the sick, a home of the emaciated, each with an unpleasant face" (VI, 241). Setsuko, not to mention Takuboku himself, was confined to bed, and Takuboku's mother, because of her own long hardships and anxieties, was exhausted and emaciated. So

Takuboku's sister Mitsuko was summoned from Hokkaido, where she had been working as an assistant to an English woman missionary.

Takuboku's mother developed tuberculosis, which took her life in March of the following year. She had quite probably caught the disease from her son, who had contracted it within two months of leaving the hospital. Setsuko was eventually infected also. Yet there was no money with which to buy medicine. Toki came to his friend's aid, arranging for the publication of the second collection of tanka, *Sad Toys*. The publisher gave an advance on the royalties, which was used to purchase medicine; but all the kindness of Toki and the generosity of the publisher were in vain. Takuboku's illness continued to worsen and it was only a matter of days before he, too, was gone. Takuboku died on April 13, 1912. His funeral, held two days later, was a gathering of distinguished writers, among them Natsume Sōseki, Sasaki Nobutsuna, Kinoshita Mokutarō and Morita Sōhei. Takuboku was twenty-six years old.

CHAPTER 2

Inkstand on a Table

T AKUBOKU was a born essayist who enjoyed writing about whatever captured his imagination. The style and the content of his essays have a remarkably wide range. He sometimes writes in the form of a report as if writing a minutely detailed letter ("From Shibutami Village"). Sometimes his essays take the form of a dialogue between the author and the reader, a device which he often employed in the essays written for the newspapers. Or sometimes an essay is expressed through the mouth of a persona, whose opinion on the issue treated in the essay obviously represents the author's own ("A Letter from the Forest"). At other times he uses a sophisticated style to match the sophisticated content, as in "The Ideas of Richard Wagner" and "The Present State of the Age of Repression."

The subject matter of the essays also covers a broad scope. Some essays are criticisms of contemporary literary works ("A Criticism of *Young Leaves of Grass*," "The Literary World of May"); some contain the author's personal reflections on life ("A Bunch of Autumn Grass," "The Peaceful Resort," "Sporadic Feelings and Reflections") or his critical analysis of the philosophy of Richard Wagner and Friedrich Nietzsche ("The Ideas of Richard Wagner," "One Branch on a Table"); others reveal Takuboku wrestling with such issues as the relationship between literature and politics ("The Present State of the Age of Repression"); while others record his continued efforts to grow as a thinker and as a poet ("From Yumi-chō").

Takuboku's essay writing, which began in 1902 and ended in January 1912, can be divided into two major periods. The early essays, written between 1902 and early 1907, throw light on the young Takuboku trying to overcome self-doubt and formulate a personal philosophy that would give direction to his life; the essays composed in the second period, between April, 1907, and the end of

1910, are dominated by Takuboku's interest in Naturalism, concluding with his eventual rejection of it, as powerfully argued in "The Present State of the Age of Repression." Although during the last year and a half of his life his interest in socialism revived, he did not produce any essays dealing with the philosophy of socialism. He was absorbed rather in the High Treason Incident and spent most of his time reading and copying the documents concerning the case. This chapter is therefore concerned only with the periods when he wrote those essays revealing the process by which he came to embrace socialism.

The value of Takuboku's essays lies in the fact that they illuminate the steady process of his growth as a critic not only of the literature of his time, but also of Japanese society as a whole. The gradual shift of emphasis manifest in the essays of each period reveals a clear pattern of change in Takuboku's interest as a writer, a pattern that parallels the progress of his maturation as a thinker. In the following pages, we shall examine selected representative essays in chronological order so that we can trace this development.

I Early Essays: The Awakening of Romanticism

Takuboku's early essays clearly show his youthful infatuation with the most popular school of thought prevailing in Japan in those days: Romanticism. The development of Romanticism in Japan owes a great deal to two important writers, Mori Ōgai (1862–1922) and Kitamura Tōkoku (1868–1894), who introduced Japanese readers to the works of such western Romantic writers as Byron, Heine, Goethe and Emerson. A German-trained physician, Mori brought back to Japan valuable first-hand knowledge of European literature and made a significant contribution to Japanese literature. He introduced Byron, for example, through a translation of a passage from *Manfred* in *The Visage* (1899), a collection of translations of western poets he himself edited. In the following year he wrote *The Dancing Girl*, his first novel, about a young Japanese government official studying in Germany who falls in love with a German show girl. Caught in the conflict between his strong love for the young woman and his duty to his country, he slowly awakens to an individualism that contradicts the demands of his feudalistic society. This novel is regarded as the first treatment of the Romantic awareness of individualism in Japan.

Tōkoku ventured to write Romantic poems in the vein of Byron.

In 1889 he wrote "Song of a Prisoner," modeled after Byron's "The Prisoner of Chillon," and in 1891 he composed "Song of Elysium" after Goethe's *Faust* and Byron's *Manfred*. But his contribution is particularly noteworthy in his essays. In "The Misanthropic Poet and Woman" (1892), for example, an essay that made him famous, Tōkoku went so far as to say that the only "key to open the secret of life" and bring out what is "most sincere and truthful" in each person is love between a man and a woman. Love not only awakens one to the worth of the individual but also functions as a tool of revolt against the old conventional society obstructing the natural growth of the human mind. One year after the appearance of the essay Tōkoku founded with Shimazaki Tōson and others an influential literary magazine, *The Literary World*, published for five years until 1898, which Tōkoku used as a channel for his criticism. The Japanese literary world of the 1890s was thus the decade of the Romantic awakening of individualism.

As shown above, the most distinctive aspect of Japanese Romanticism is that it was regarded as synonymous with individualism. This trend became more narrowly channeled toward the turn of the century, intensified by the introduction of Nietzsche to Japanese readers. One significant early contribution was the essay by Anezaki Chūfū, "The Importing of Neitzschean Philosophy and Buddhism," which appeared in 1898. This was followed in 1899 by Yoshida Seiichi's "Nietzsche's Philosophy." Two years later Takayama Chogyū published his article "The Writer as a Critic of Civilization," in which he presented Nietzsche as the most important critic of Western civilization. Nietzschean individualism and the Nietzschean view of man and his place in society gained a strong hold on young intellectuals. The young Takuboku, already strongly individualistic and ready to absorb anything new and dynamic, was receptive to Nietzsche's ideas as set forth in Takayama's writings. Though Takuboku, as well as other young intellectuals, was to reject Nietzsche almost as soon as he accepted him, his encounter with the great thinker left its mark. It is hardly an exaggeration to say that Takuboku's view of life in his late teens owes much to Nietzschean romantic individualism.

Takuboku's existential inquiry into the nature of the self, which clearly reflects the influence of Nietzsche's philosophy, begins rather early. The first reference to the question of self-identity appears in a letter to Nomura Kodō, dated September 17, 1903:

When, after painstaking inner struggle day and night, I finally began to grasp what the self is and what composes man, the degree of my indifference to the world increased. When we can manifest the component of the self with far-reaching compassion and love, the praises and reproaches of the world cease to be our concern. He who is most faithful to the self—is he not also truthful to others? There exists a drastic difference between my egoism and individualism (so called). He who has a genuine love for himself ought to love others universally. (VII, 29–30)

Takuboku's intellectual pursuit of the worth of the individual is further illustrated by his attempt at formulating a religious view of life in his own terms. He intuitively recognizes that self-knowledge cannot be separated from the knowledge of something that is the origin of the self. As he understood it, consciousness of the individual self leads ultimately to a spiritual awareness: "When one inquires into the nature of the self, one comes to realize that the great human will in the end aspires to respond to the needs of spiritual life and that it not only expands the self but unifies both the subject and the object, while embracing the eternal world wholeheartedly. When this realization inspires one's heart like a flash of lightning, faith and hope will be founded on firm ground" (VII, 31). Takuboku in "The Peaceful Resort" further has this to say:

The self existing beyond one's consciousness has deep roots in the center of the universe. It is called by different names such as God, Buddha and the primary will. One differs from others in facial features and character, yet once one enters the region of the spirit, one reaches at once the state of selflessness. The small self, namely the self of matter, is unified with the larger Self, the Self of the Spirit. The union is not the death of the self but its extension into the eternal infinite universe through a complete liberation from every distinction, time and space. (IV, 76)

Takuboku's view that the individual self can achieve a transcendental union with a higher self parallels the conventional view of various mystical traditions and is not an original idea. What one sees here is that though it might be merely an intellectual exercise, Takuboku at least tried to elevate his vision of life and man, thereby enabling himself to observe life from a higher dimension of consciousness. For Takuboku this experience of spiritual union would not call for self-effacement; in this sense he was a true Romantic. The self-confidence, outspokenness and defiance of society shown in his later essays spring from his strong conviction concerning the merits of individualism.

Takuboku's ideal then was to formulate a philosophy that would enable him to demonstrate his concern for others while maintaining his own distinct individuality. He was introduced to Christianity through Tsunajima Ryōsen, but interpreted the faith as leading to a loss of individual identity. In the essay, "In Memory of Tsunajima Ryōsen," Takuboku writes:

Life is composed of two phases. . . . Where are these phases grounded? They are founded on two desires of life. What are the two desires? They are the will to develop one's self and the will to unify the self and others. In my estimation, one possesses these wills in one's character. In short, the basic essence of the universe is made of these two wills. . . . Ryōsen has chosen one phase of life: to return to God, whereas I select another. Herein lies the reason why I could not understand, sympathize with nor accept his view. (IV, 121)

The idea set forth in this essay Takuboku calls "the supreme thought" at this point in his career. Life is then a continuing process of self-development along with the extension of one's sympathetic imagination; and the purpose of man's existence is to create what Takuboku calls "a wholesome individuality," which is possible only when a person can integrate these divergent strivings. Life is essentially dynamic: it enables man to continue to create a new self with a better knowledge of the value of life gained through personal struggle. As Takuboku says elsewhere:

I am afraid that by trusting that individuality is something already fixed, that is, "a given fact," we do not realize how stagnant we are making our thinking. History reveals the trend of a certain indefinite will of mankind. Similarly, a person's whole life reveals the trend and direction of his will. For those living, there exists only the will and its propensity, and never is it stationary. What is called the self or individuality is fluid, something containing perfectability that must be nourished and realized. I believe that that something cannot be recognized as a form while one is alive, that is, while one vigorously maintains spiritual activities. I believe that the ideas I mentioned before—the improvement, the unification and completeness of one's life—are in fact the synonyms for "the making of the self." (VII, 293)

Hence the mission of a thinker who is sensitive to the *Zeitgeist*: "Our ideal is to realize the age of the liberated self, our calling is to fight for the emancipation of the self" (V, 177). The philosophy that Takuboku worked out in this early period was to make him subsequently receptive to the Naturalistic movement and to socialism, both of which were strong proponents of individualism.

A. "The Ideas of Richard Wagner"

Examined in the context of Takuboku's formulating his unique philosophy of life, such pieces as "The Ideas of Richard Wagner" and "A Letter from the Forest" hold a significant place among his early essays. The former represents Takuboku's definition of the mission of man in life, and the latter the definition of education as a means to equip one for the mission. "The Ideas of Richard Wagner," Takuboku's ambitious attempt at synthesizing his understanding of Wagner's philosophy, which promptly superseded his interest in Nietzsche's, in many respects helped him develop his own life view. The essay was left incomplete, having been abandoned when Takuboku realized the immensity of the subject. But it is a culmination of Takuboku's endeavor to come to terms with the question of the self.

Takuboku first became interested in Wagner in 1903, when he was forced by illness to return to Shibutami from Tokyo. In a letter dated January 13, 1904, he wrote to Anezaki:

In the fall of the year [1902], hoping to develop myself in the world of combat, I left the school at Morioka in the middle of the school year, and aimlessly began to live the life of a wanderer in the dust of the capital. . . . Yet it was last spring when the snow was still deep that with heavy pain of heart, accompanied with suffering from illness, I had to return home to rest my defeated body. After I came back, still in anguish and sorrow, the first thing that occurred to me was the possibility of studying Richard Wagner, whom I came to know through your book. (VII, 35)

The study of Wagner done by Anezaki to which Takuboku refers is the essay, "In Answer to Takayama Chogyū," which appeared in the February and March issues of *The Sun* in 1902. Takuboku's grasp of the essence of Wagner's philosophy is succinctly summed up in his diary:

In the philosophy that undergirds Wagner's operas I have discovered a basic element very compatible with my sensibility: it is his poignant world view of love as the expansion of the human will. Influenced though he was by Schopenhauer, he did not fall a prey to the fallacy of "the extinction of the will" as Tolstoy did, nor was he carried away by the extremity of Nietzschean "expansion of the will." It is his genius that enabled him to make a great subtle discovery of truth in the middle of these two opposing views. It is the beatific state in which mortals shake hands with the gods, realized only through the heroic courage inherent in love as the expansion of will. Thus all the heroes in Wagner's works are the warriors of this ideal. For these heroes there exist only love and battle with no moments for reflection on life and death. The whole life of Wagner has best exemplified the life of such a brave hero. The great impact I received from Wagner's precept is indeed inestimable. (VII, 111–12)

Wagner's perfect balance of Nietzsche and Tolstoy united the individual will with love for others, individualism and altruism. It is this ideal, precipitated from the fusion of the minds of two great thinkers who maintained completely opposite views of man's place in life, that Takuboku wished to bring out in the essay "The Ideas of Richard Wagner."

"The Ideas of Richard Wagner" was published in the *Iwate Daily News* for seven days from the end of May to early June, 1903. According to Takuboku's introduction, his first intention was to serialize a work of comprehensive scope. He had planned to construct the essay in eight major sections. To quote some of the plan:

  I. Introduction: the nineteenth century and Wagner—the ideals of civilization—the quarrel of man with the gods—individualism—the world harmonized by Love—implications of Wagner (comprehensive criticism)

  II. Wagner's personality: his character and various accomplishments—the foundation of his philosophy

  III. Wagner's political ideas: the ideal for a nation—the foundation of the national will and its absolute power—Wagner and Germany—the liberation of the race and the reform of mankind—the destruction of the ideal of the modern state—Wagner and socialism

  IV. Wagner's religion: what is religion?—Wagner and Christ and Christianity—studies in ancient Greek culture—religion and the arts—Wagner's religous sentiment and his two great beliefs. (IV, 16)

One can easily see that the issue Takuboku chose was too large for him to deal with in a newspaper essay. It is no surprise that he did not complete the work; he undoubtedly realized that even though he could grasp the essence of Wagner's philosophy, a complete critical analysis of it was beyond his capacity. What was written is, however, enough to show the clarity of insight and the soundness of judgment of this youth of eighteen.

After introducing Richard Wagner as a great prophet of the time, Takuboku gives a succinct summary of the intellectual and moral condition of western man in the nineteenth century. He maintains that although man has been liberated from the confining, superstitious old faith of the Middle Ages, he is currently enslaved by an obsession with the physical world, which he has turned to in an attempt to fill his spiritual void. This obsession with the physical world has given rise to an excessive emphasis on materialism, which threatens to obscure the dignity of man, which is his spirituality. As a result, modern man has begun to lose his aspiration to return to the prime source of life. Intellect, traditionally a supplementary faculty for man's spiritual aspiration, has long lost its primary function and has been employed instead in the creation of an all-pervading conventionalism stifling individual freedom. Consequently the heart and will of society have continued to decline. Compounding the problem is a rapidly developing individualism that has become too powerful for society to come to terms with. What man must recognize, then, is: "No matter how useful the key of intellect or no matter how intense the excitement aroused by the arts, the cultivation of them is of little value if one's life and heart fail to open the vast gate of faith that stands at the palace of the spiritual region, the ultimate utopia, and trust to the assistance of something outside oneself so as to let one enjoy the glory of eternal bliss" (IV, 17). In short, one must perceive the basic nature of man: man is essentially a spiritual and moral being. Takuboku maintains that Tolstoy and Nietzsche are the two giants of the nineteenth century who made their age aware of the potential of man as a spiritual being.

Takuboku comprehends Nietzsche's Superman as a personification of the human will: "His so-called Superman is indeed the personification of the incomparable power of will with which he, in order to create a life most congenial to his personal values, denies not only morality, history and civilization but also all other human beings except himself—in short, without remorse he drives with a curse from this world anyone who stands in his way and continues single-mindedly an unresting striving, never hesitating to use his savage force whenever necessary" (IV, 20).

Takuboku perceives a subtle distinction, however, between the

Nietzschean concept of the Superman and individualism; and he argues that the world fails to see the difference. He believes that Nietzsche's philosophy is a glorification of thinly disguised, unruly egoism and that the flaws as well as the limitations of Nietzscheanism need to be spelled out.

Takuboku sees that while Nietzsche portrays one extreme, that of egoistic self-affirmation, Tolstoy represents the other extreme, that of complete negation of the individual self:

According to his belief, man created by the divine will is made in such a way that by nature he cannot fulfill his desires in this phenomenal world. In short, Tolstoy is a believer in original sin. . . . All the disturbances of peace and the insecurity and suffering in the world come from the collision bet-ween a man's attempt to carry out his desires, an attempt which is impossi-ble to fulfill, and God's absolute will. In order to build a society that suits God's will by avoiding the greatest unhappiness of mankind, in other words, in order for all mankind to construct the most ideal world for their exis-tence, man must create a serene paradise of total equality while burying his free will deep in the earth. (IV, 21)

But no matter how philosophically sound or how dynamic the argu-ments, Takuboku can accept neither Tolstoy's self-abnegating humanism nor Nietzsche's self-asserting superhumanism, for Takuboku's ideal, like Wagner's, lies in the reconciliation of the two opposite views: "Man is neither a creature existing only in the di-mension of so-called Reality like a god nor that of various forms existing only in the world of phenomena. The ultimate purpose of his existence is to infiltrate into both of these regions and create harmony between them" (IV, 21–22).

Takuboku completed a mere one-tenth of his original plan; but from what he did develop, the reader can get a glimpse of his intellectual precocity in his analysis of the conflicting views of man. He performed, or at least attempted to perform, an enormous labor of scholarship through which to formulate his view of man and of life in general. Yet Takuboku was not just a theorist; he wanted to see this ideal realized in actual life, first in his own character and then, through his influence, in the lives of others. Education, he believed, was the one indispensable means to achieve this ideal, and his at-tempt at establishing his own theory of education in this context is best shown in "A Letter from the Forest."

B. *"A Letter from the Forest"*

"A Letter from the Forest" was published on March 1, 1907, in the *Morioka Middle School Alumni Magazine*. Takuboku wrote this essay to present his views on the contemporary state of Japanese education, particularly on the elementary level. However, as the education of the young is an expression of the current philosophy of the society of which they are a part, Takuboku leads the essay to his main concern, which is to bring about substantial changes, social as well as moral, in Japanese society. He is especially critical of the strong nationalistic sentiment of a society drunk with the sweetness of victory over Russia.

The opening paragraphs give the impression that Takuboku himself does not consider his essay to be a serious one. Introducing himself as a part time teacher in a nearby village, he claims his profession to be dreaming, and his titles, self-endowed or given by others, to be "dreamer," "professor of dreams," or "a piece of stone lying idly in the grass." The first one-third of the essay is, in fact, full of such nonsensical descriptions of the writer's background, as if to convince the reader that he is merely recording the words of one talking in his sleep. The apparent humor at the beginning is, however, a thin disguise for a serious purpose: wearing the mask of a comedian is a device Takuboku uses to free his imagination from unnecessary concern about possible censorship from government officials. Once he commences to deal with his main theme, the jocose tone disappears, and his pen flows with force and style.

At the time Takuboku was writing this essay the Japanese educational system was perhaps the most advanced and democratic in the world, an institution of which the country could be justly proud. The Imperial Rescript was put forth in 1890, when Takuboku was four years old. Here Takuboku examines the place formal education holds in Japanese society in this post Russo-Japanese War era. Triumph over the giant country Russia had strengthened nationalistic sentiment, already stimulated by the victory over China ten years earlier. As this heightened sense of nationalism had determined the course of education, discussion of education provided Takuboku with an excellent opportunity to voice his concern over the direction his country was taking.

Takuboku begins the principal part of the essay by challenging the common sentiment that the victory over Russia has affirmed Japan's status as a civilized nation. Japanese take pride in the fact that their country is the only one in Asia with a constitutional government; but Takuboku questions the substance of it:

I admit that Japan is indeed a fortunate nation which has accomplished an extraordinary reformation in only fifty years. Japan is now a constitutional people. . . . However, I ask myself: Where in this constitutionalized country is there a constitutional society? How often is a constitutional act performed in front of me? Aren't only unconstitutional affairs thriving? Aren't the political parties of our country, which are supposed to represent organized political thoughts, nothing but a group put together by self-interest and ambition? Aren't the people still the ignorant masses who, like those in the age of feudalism, place the power of the government and that of money above the freedom and rights of the individual? (IV, 99)

To Takuboku the so-called modernization of Japan following the Meiji Restoration is merely a surface achievement: the prevalent notion that Japan is a world power is a false illusion. While it is true that Japan won the war against Russia, the war was a contest between Japanese and Russian military powers, not between the two cultures. Takuboku believes that Japan has gained its reputation as a world power only in terms of its military strength. Military victory has not helped to advance the true modernization of Japan, which, Takuboku maintains, must be based upon respect for and freedom of the individual. In this respect Takuboku holds that the Russo-Japanese War has perhaps worked against Japan's moderization; at the very least it has certainly failed to develop it.

The root of the failure, Takuboku feels, is in the minds of the Japanese people, molded for centuries by the old feudalistic frame of thought. With the conventional mentality formed by this highly regimented feudalism the Japanese are incapable of absorbing individual freedom:

Ah, readers! I fear that ten years ago when the Japanese had just waked up from a long night's dream, the time was not ripe for us to receive the most valuable gift of freedom. Can we not liken the situation ten years ago to a small boy, who, having just finished the initiation ceremony, is allowed to put on the treasured family armor and made to carry a six-foot long spear? He puts on the armor and carries the spear, knowing nothing about their worth nor use; in short, he is not yet ready for them. The Japanese wear the clothes of modern civilization; the Russians have digested it deep in their stomachs. (IV, 103)

Takuboku recognized the hypocrisy in the so-called modernization of Japan, which was in fact a disguise for the fabrication of imperialism under the undisputed authority of the emperor. One can catch here already the first rumblings of Takuboku's eventual conflict with nationalism, the argument of which is fully discussed in "The Present State of the Age of Repression," written three years after "A Letter from the Forest."

In a country where freedom is suppressed a Tolstoy is born, but in a country where freedom is guaranteed by its constitution no champion of individual freedom is produced. Realizing this paradox, Takuboku has assumed the responsibility of appealing to the audience as one rare apologist of freedom.

The last third of the essay concerns itself with Takuboku's theory of education, a philosophy which is derived, as Takuboku explains, from his own personal experience. True education, he argues, cannot be obtained in Japan's rigidly regimented school system, though it is, Takuboku admits, the best system available in the East. Education must be a means to develop a pupil's independent spirit and his sensitivity to life in accord with the gradual maturation of his inquiring mind. In short:

> The supreme purpose of education is to nurture a genius, to create a person who can contribute to the history of the world. Then the second goal is to produce a healthy people who will believe it their mission to follow and respect such a genius. . . . In other words, the true purpose of education is to make men, not to create scholars, engineers, office workers, teachers, merchants, farmers or government officers. Solely to produce human beings, this is enough. Conferring knowledge occupies only a small portion of true education. (IV, 107)

Examined from this point of view it becomes apparent that current Japanese education is dominated by educationalists complacent in the security of formal structures guided by self-interest rather than concern for the welfare and growth of the pupils in their charge. Put another way, teachers have become machines the function of which is to process the material—the pupils—automatically. Forms of education exist—but with no substance in them. Therefore Takuboku concludes: "Japanese education is a splendid building inhabited by no man; . . . it is the mummy of education. It is a guillotine that slaughters genius, a land of indolence removed from real life" (IV, 108–9).

In "A Letter from the Forest" Takuboku, particularizing the problems of the current educational system, has merely set forth his educational theory without touching upon a possible practical way to implement the philosophy; he was after all required to conform to the word limit set by the editor of the magazine. However, considering the fact that Takuboku while teaching at Shibutami secured the permission of his principal to put pupils in charge of the farewell party for the graduating class in the spring of 1907 (they wrote letters of invitation and planned the program), one can see that his educational theory was more than the insubstantial talk of a dreamer. It had been tested through application and was confirmed by his genuine concern for the place of education in modern Japan for the creation of a better future.

II *Later Essays*

A. *The End of Romanticism: "One Branch on a Table"*

Takuboku's early essays are dominated by his youthful enthusiasm and idealization of Romanticism, as a passionate advocate of individualism or as a theorist of education. As he continued to confront difficulties in his daily life, however, his perspective on life changed accordingly, and, in turn, modified his literary taste. From Romanticism he turned to Naturalism. Takuboku's initial interest in Naturalism dates back to a brief stay in Tokyo in 1906. His desire to experiment with the Naturalistic novel increased in direct proportion to the frustration he faced because of the necessity of providing financial security for his family during his year in Hokkaido.

Naturalism had a special appeal to Takuboku; his own experience had led him to form a similar view of life, with a similar positive acceptance of individualism. What he found good in the movement is expressed in this passage from "One Branch on a Table": "Naturalism, born as a result of the development of self-consciousness . . . is a movement that brings all living things back to the most natural state" (IV, 133). He accepted Naturalism as a literary movement as well as a philosophical one, a movement that would break through Japanese literary conventions as well as traditional Japanese ways of thinking. To the Takuboku of 1906 and 1907 Naturalism appeared to be a movement that put the spirit of freedom to the fore, and he embraced it enthusiastically.

Yet as manifested in "One Branch on a Table" Takuboku's attitude toward Naturalism in 1908 is less zealous: he increasingly grows skeptical of the validity of the movement. His uneasiness about it can be seen first in his letter to Miyazaki Ikuu, written about the same time as "One Branch on a Table": "The rise of Naturalism illuminates the fact that deep in the hearts of the people today nihilism is taking hold. The only message Naturalism has for people is: 'Let it be.' Neither good nor evil, nor beauty nor ugliness, only 'That's the way it is.' The way it is! What a depressing expression that is!" (VII, 178). This statement is a close paraphrase of the central idea of the essay: "When one deprives life of all 'life illusions,' one sinks into the sorrow associated with the exposure of reality. This sorrow is a sadness without tears, for one sees only 'nothing' when utterly separated from all illusions. Within the bounds of 'nothing' there exist no passions, no tears, only silence" (IV, 132). Though acknowledging Naturalism as an important literary and philosophical movement, Takuboku now gives it only half-hearted acceptance. He senses, though vaguely, that Naturalism has an inherent flaw which he cannot accept. As Takuboku analyzes it in the essay, his uneasiness comes from the fact that its emphasis on photographic realism rejects a "life-illusion" that gives color to human life and gives birth to hope, an illusion Takuboku considers necessary for man's existence. His reservations concerning the Naturalistic movement, however, are not yet serious enough for him to totally repudiate it at this point: as soon as he is settled in Tokyo a few months after writing "One Branch on a Table" he is absorbed in experimentation with Naturalistic novels such as *The Hospital Window* and "Dysentery." Takuboku's final severance from the kind of Naturalism represented by its leading exponents in Japan comes after he undergoes a severe inner struggle in the spring of 1909, a subject to be examined later.

In "One Branch on a Table" Takuboku again deals with Nietzsche. This second extensive treatment of the philosopher has no significantly new interpretation, but there is an attitude markedly different from the one expressed five years earlier. The tone of the essay suggests that Takuboku has developed a deep skepticism regarding egoistic philosophy. In "The Ideas of Richard Wagner" Takuboku evaluated Nietzsche in relation to Wagner and Tolstoy without examining him independently; but now five years later Takuboku has come to feel that Nietzsche's philosophy, however

dynamic and influential for the development of modern individualism, has failed in resolving the contradiction between
idealism and the actuality of life, the former beginning to lose its
attraction in proportion to his preoccupation with the latter.
Takuboku could not embrace Nietzsche wholeheartedly not only
because he was not comfortable with egoism but because he had
begun to doubt the feasibility of any philosophy's ability to understand life, the basic nature of which is to Takuboku unpredictability:
"After all, what is the use of knowledge? Man always attempts to
govern himself, yet he is always governed by something other than
himself. That something ultimately remains unidentifiable. We
neither know its face nor hear its voice. Although we inquire of the
goddess of wisdom concerning its identity, she remains silent, telling us nothing" (IV, 137). The conflict taking place in his mind is the
conflict between his dream and reality, between what he thought
was the answer to his existence, a philosophical quest for life's
meaning, and what actual life demands. When Takuboku comes to
the awareness that life's requirements will constantly thwart the
realization of his ideals, he becomes disillusioned and skeptical of
the view of life he has formed and of philosophies similar to his own.
His skepticism is so intense as to verge on nihilism: "In this world,
there is no ideal that is built on unshakable ground. In other words,
there exists no true hope in human life" (VII, 234). One can see that
Takuboku's early ponderings were concerned with the question of
human autonomy, but within five years the focus of his thinking has
changed from metaphysical to empirical concerns. Let us look,
then, at the record of the beginning of this change, a record kept not
in essays but in a diary, Takuboku's *The Rōmaji Diary*.

B.   *The End of Romanticism:* The Rōmaji Diary

Takuboku's diary, which he kept from April 7 to June 1, 1909, is
today commonly known as *The Rōmaji Diary* because he wrote it
in *rōmaji*, a system of transliteration of the Japanese syllabary which
was still relatively new. It presents a candid account of the inner
struggle that hastened his maturity as a writer and a thinker. The
painful experiences recorded in the diary helped him to develop
insight into the value of human life and his individual existence, the
insight revealed in various writings produced between late 1909 and
the end of 1910. This period of maturation must have included those

months during and immediately following *The Rōmaji Diary*. Takuboku's experimentation with *rōmaji* not only helped him in his personal development but also offered a possibility for a new literary genre. For this reason *The Rōmaji Diary* holds a significant place in the bulk of modern Japanese literature as well as in Takuboku's complete works.

The Rōmaji Diary reveals a young man vacillating between hope and despair, between the desire for individual achievement and crippling self-doubt. Moreover, he is further frustrated by family obligations, which impose a strict limit on the extent to which he can devote himself to the pursuit of his ideals. The double burden of financial need and failure as a novelist weighs heavily upon him, sharpening his senses now operating on the extreme edge of despair. It is Takuboku's honest recording of his inner life, however, that gives power and artistic unity to the diary. *The Rōmaji Diary* is more than a diary. Takuboku has unwittingly made it a kind of Naturalistic novel, the hero of which is himself.

Takuboku's dejection is rooted in his feeling of guilt at neglecting his family. He had promised Miyazaki in Hakodate that he would call his family to Tokyo within six months, but the term had now long expired. Takuboku complains incessantly of being short of money, but when he obtains any, he spends it recklessly. Thanks to the generosity of the editor of the *Asahi* newspaper he had secured a job as a proofreader in March, the income from which was sufficient to support his family; but instead of sending for them immediately he keeps spending the money on books, expensive meals, and, most of all, on prostitutes. Takuboku worries not so much about how soon he should call his family as about his own reluctance even to correspond with them: "Right now I should be writing to Mother and the others, but I dread it, too. I'm always wanting to write about anything that might please them in order to comfort them. I haven't forgotten my mother or my wife. No, I've been thinking of them every day. Yet I've mailed only one letter and one postcard since the beginning of the year" (VI, 136). It is clear that in this entry Takuboku is evading the real issue. Whether through choice or from necessity, the young man still searching for his own path in life has been weighed down with too many responsibilities. He is now enjoying a welcome respite from the burden. Looking back at the year before, he remarks: "The summer at Seki-shin-kan [his lodging house]! It was the summer when, in spite of financial difficulties, I

was happy to be free from family obligations even for half a year.
Right! It was the time when I enjoyed being a semi-bachelor, paying
little attention to my family" (VI, 151). Having once put off the
heavy load, Takuboku cannot summon the self-discipline to pick it
up again: "I've put on now the heavy, heavy clothes,/ The clothes of
responsibility./ If I could take them off—Ah!/ How enrapturing!/ My
body would be as light as hydrogen,/ Flying high up into the vast
sky./ The crowd below would cry out:/ 'A skylark!' Ah!" (VI, 133)

Takuboku at one point attempts to solve his dilemma by imagina-
tively sketching the character he wishes to be. Speaking of himself
in the third person, he says: "Stripping himself of all the armor of
restrictions and conventions, he, 'the mighty one', fought bravely
singlehandedly. With an iron heart, with no tears or smiles on his
face, he advanced straight toward the objective of his desires, taking
no notice of things around him. Abandoning everything called vir-
tue as if it were dust, the brave one performed without regret what
no other human would dare" (VI, 129). Yet these courageous acts
are performed only in the mind of the writer. Takuboku recognizes
the vanity of what he has written, which in turn increases his anguish: "One hundred days have passed by [since the New Year
began] while my body in armor trembled in great anticipation.
Whom did I conquer? How strong did I become?" (VI, 129).
Takuboku is too gentlehearted to be an aggressive, egoistic fighter;
furthermore, he is too sensitive to sacrifice his family completely for
a personal goal. His anxiety for his family is magnified in proportion
to his increasing desire to be free from his obligations to them.
Takuboku describes what in his imagination he saw while riding a
streetcar on his way to work one day:

I saw a little girl three years old or so. Kyōko came immediately to my
mind. Setsuko leaves for work in the morning and returns in the evening.
While she is gone, Mother and Kyōko stay alone in the small, cramped
house. Ah, grandmother and granddaughter! Thinking about their daily life
brings tears to my eyes. Food is the only pleasure for the child. When she
becomes bored with the monotonous, somber day, Kyōko will surely ask for
something to eat. But there's nothing to eat! "Grandma, Kyō-chan wants
something to eat! Grandma," Kyōko begs, weeping in hunger. Even
Grandma's kind words cannot console the child. "Here, here . . . ," says
Grandma. Ah, a piece of pickled radish! (VI, 146)

The struggle to resolve the conflicting feelings toward his family has
quickened Takuboku's imagination.

Takuboku's melancholy develops also from his failure to achieve recognition as a novelist. Despite publishers' constant rejections of his work, Takuboku is too proud to give up his desire to be accepted as a novelist. He frequently excuses himself from work at the newspaper office in order to spend the day writing a story, but he seldom gets beyond the first two pages. His attempt to write is always met with frustration: "I was determined to write something today and I didn't go to work. No, since I didn't want to work, I decided to write. At any rate, I tried to write a story, 'Red Ink,' which I had thought out last night. It's a story about my suicide. I wrote about three pages or so, but I couldn't go any further.

Why can't I write? I can't look at myself objectively. No, I just can't write. I can't think clearly" (VI, 144). Repeated failures at last lead him to admit defeat: "I had to seriously consider the fact that I simply can't write a novel. I had to concede that there's no hope for my future" (VI, 143).

The sense of failure as a writer added to his sense of failure as a son, husband and father leaves Takuboku with the feeling of complete failure as a man. In *The Rōmaji Diary* one comes across entry after entry expressing existential fear:

I said to myself, "I will give up my literary career." "If I give up literature, what shall I do?" Death! . . . Really, what should I do? Is there anything left for me?

My heart was like a sick bird flapping its wings in an attempt to keep itself from plunging into the pit of darkness.

A useless key! That's it! No matter where I carry it, I can't find a hole the key fits. (VI, 145, 159, 169)

Finding no satisfactory answer to the question of his place in life, Takuboku finds a temporary escape in wishful thinking. He fantasizes finding an empty house, where he can sleep as long as he wants; he dreams of riding a train just to be riding; he imagines going either to an isolated place where no other human being can be seen or else to a place jammed with people, such as a movie house, to be lost among the crowd; or, naively believing that illness will liberate him from the burdens of life, he dreams of escape through sickness: "For one year, or even one month,/ Or a week, or three days,/ God, if you exist, O God,/ My wish is only one: Batter my body!/ Painful though it may be, I don't care./ Grant me illness!" (VI, 132) The irony is that two years later this wish comes true, and a

fatal sickness emancipates him from all the burdens of the world.
But at the present time, as Takuboku knows well, all these fantasies
serve merely to increase his frustration over his confinement by
family obligations as well as to intensify the awareness that the
freedom he yearns for is only an illusion: "I can neither go to a place
where no other humans exist nor discover satisfaction with them.
Unable to endure the pain of life, I know no way to cope with life
itself. All human relations are shackles and responsibility creeps in.
Hamlet said: 'To be, or, not to be'; but today the question of death
has become more complicated than in Hamlet's day" (VI, 132).

Takuboku cannot conquer despair, but one can observe that his
agony has done him a favor. The struggle with despondency has led
him to formulate his own view of the writer's responsibility to society: "The writer must be a critic, or at least a reformer, of life, not a
mere observer of it" (VI, 127–28). Takuboku has developed also the
capacity to empathize with the suffering of others. In one dark
account of his hardship, a single incident recorded stands out as a
glimmer of light. He writes about an unexpected encounter with
two youths from the country: one is from Takuboku's home village,
Shibutami, the other from Tokushima Prefecture. Takuboku feels
immediate empathy with them; from his own tormenting experience in Tokyo he knows very well what awaits them: "Lured by the
flame, summer insects burn themselves to death. These youths,
deluded by the apparent glory of city life, drove themselves to it
without realizing what the consequences would be. Only one alternative is left for them, either to be burned to death or to fly away"
(VI, 165). Takuboku helps them find a lodging place, treats them to
meals and even offers financial help, all the while neglecting his own
family suffering greater hardships. Takuboku seems to be showing
off his kindness in order to impress the boys from the country. Yet
his generosity to the young men should not be interpreted mainly as
a display of vanity. His kindness is genuine, and this act of compassion helps him regain a sense of his own worth. His taking pity on
the youths functions as a vicarious expiation of the guilt he feels
toward his family.

The Rōmaji Diary closes with a record of Takuboku's reunion with
his family and their moving into the upstairs of a barber shop.
Miyazaki has taken pity on them and paid their way to Tokyo. This
compulsory reunion, however, works favorably for Takuboku, for he
is now bound to think of his family first, making it necessary for him

to abandon his excessive introspection. This release from self-interrogation brings him to a higher level of objectivity which eventually enables him to mature in his perception of the function of literature in life and, more important, in his understanding of his own place as a man of letters.

But why was the diary a *"rōmaji"* diary? Takuboku's reason for writing the diary in *rōmaji* calls for clarification. At the beginning of the diary he explains: "Why, then, have I decided to write this diary in *rōmaji*? Why? I love my wife and because I love her, I don't want her to read this diary. This is a lie! While it's true that I love her and I don't want her to read this, these two facts are not necessarily related" (VI, 120–21). Takuboku's rationale is odd indeed, for his wife had studied English and could undoubtedly read *rōmaji*. It seems that we should look for the true motive in another direction. As we have seen, whenever Takuboku tries to write a story, he cannot get beyond the first two or three pages. Preoccupied with his problems, he is unable to objectify his experience. Takuboku, then, has used *rōmaji* as a means of looking at himself from a distance, of objectifying his intense emotional experience. Putting his experience down on paper has released his tension and using *rōmaji* has helped him to achieve greater detachment.

Further, using *rōmaji* freed Takuboku from the conventional literary forms associated with both Japanese and Chinese characters, which helped him develop the self-discipline manifested in his simple refined style.[1] That Takuboku enjoyed this stylistic freedom is most apparent in his vivid descriptions of various individuals sketched in the diary. Takuboku's realistic portrayals, nurtured during his apprenticeship to Naturalism, give us the living human beings: his friend Kindaichi, the housemaids at his lodging house, the two youths from the country, various prostitutes who provide him with brief moments of physical gratification; the list goes on. As a result Takuboku's diary resembles a novel. In fact, though the form is that of a diary, it is more like an autobiographical-confessional novel, the genre started by Tayama Katai, the champion of the Japanese Naturalistic movement. The protagonist of *The Rōmaji Diary* is a man struggling alone against the wretchedness of life about which he tells the reader with honesty. The protagonist is real because in him Takuboku has presented himself without speciousness, exactly as he felt and thought. Takuboku's friends and acquaintances function as minor characters who serve to shed light on the

character of the protagonist and on the intensity of his inner struggle. His daily factual entry then is the development of plot in which
the whole history of the protagonist's inner life is told with realism
and exactness of feeling. Revitalizing the old genre of diary with a
new approach of writing in *rōmaji* and with a new emphasis on
dramatizing his inner life, Takuboku has made *The Rōmaji Diary* a
unique literary record of his personal development both as a writer
and as a thinker.

C. *Rejection of Naturalism: "Sporadic Feelings and Reflections"*

The painful inner struggle brought Takuboku to a vantage point
from which he could survey life and the function of literature with
greater clarity. His perception now focused on real life, he could see
the flaws of Naturalism more distinctly. Such essays as "From
Yumi-chō: Poems to Eat" (November-December, 1909), "Sporadic
Feelings and Reflections" (December, 1909) and "Hasty Ideas"
(February, 1910) reflect Takuboku's maturity and confidence in his
view of himself as a writer and a thinker. The shift in his view of
literature is best revealed in his rejection of Naturalism, which
tended to separate literature from life. Of the essays cited above,
"From Yumi-chō" is an important document for understanding
Takuboku's unique poetic theory, and it will be referred to in the
proper context in the next chapter. "Hasty Ideas," an essay in which
Takuboku succinctly defines the "modernity" of Japan as nothing
but hastiness in judgment, is a valuable essay in itself. But since it is
not directly related to Takuboku's philosophy of art and life, which is
our central concern, it is excluded from the present study. Let us
here narrow our focus on "Sporadic Feelings and Reflections," the
essay which laid the foundation for "The Present State of the Age of
Repression," written eight months later.

As the title of the essay suggests, "Sporadic Feelings and Reflections" treats a variety of subjects and is written by and large in a
casual fashion. It includes such topics as an encounter with an old
man, criticism of novels of Mori Ōgai, Shimazaki Tōson and Tayama
Katai and their narrative technique, and observations on the fad-
dishness of "modern" Japanese people. All these subjects are handled with a light, relaxed tone and an underlying seriousness. The
real importance of the essay, however, lies in the fact that Takuboku
devotes about one third of it to expressing his dissatisfaction with
the Naturalistic movement.

Takuboku's rejection of the doctrines preached by the Naturalists was not done in haste. As can be seen from the discussion of "One Branch on a Table," it was the consequence of a gradual and steady change in himself. Various writings during 1908 and 1910 illustrate this. In his diary dated May 8, 1908, for example, Takuboku says: "I endorse Naturalism, but I am not a Naturalist" (V, 259). A few months later, writing to a friend he remarks: "I approve of Naturalism; yet I cannot agree with those who believe that it is the only ideal" (VII, 255). His disillusionment with Naturalism increases in proportion to his growing conviction concerning the function of art in society. In short, Takuboku now sees in 1909 that the writer should make a conscious effort to close the gap between literature and life, for the artist is a critic of life whose responsibility it is to advance an alternative for the reform of life through his works:

The short stories of these days have become almost like word painting; at least we cannot help feeling that way when we read them. That we are dissatisfied with them shows that Naturalism as a philosophy of life has gradually lost its influence.

Times have changed! No one denies that Naturalism was the philosophy we used to pursue most earnestly, but we discovered somehow a contradiction of logic in its theory. When we pressed forward beyond the contradiction, the sword in our hands had ceased to be the sword of Naturalism; at least I, for one, could no longer remain content with the attitude of objectivity. The writer's approach to life should not be one of detachment: he must be a critic, or otherwise a reformer, of life. (VI, 127–28)

The writer, then, should have a strong moral commitment to social reform. One can see that Takuboku's moralistic view of the writer's mission in life is a modification of his Romantic view of a thinker's responsibility: to realize the age of the emancipated self. The view is now substantiated with his personal life experience, which has enabled him to confirm his old belief. In order to discharge his responsibility then, as Takuboku has said elsewhere, the writer must reform himself first: "In order to thoroughly discipline and govern ourselves and to improve our life through discovering a just way by which to move forward, must we not first reflect on ourselves and our way of life?" (IV, 240). Takuboku sees life as a continuum of reflection, self-reform and self-improvement, an individual process requiring individual freedom. He has therefore begun to perceive the country's nationalistic philosophy, stressing the individual's total

dedication to national goals, as a great hindrance to individual development. The Naturalists, by refusing to look beyond the strictly
private world of the individual, have become blind to the threat to
that world. That they did not recognize that their practice con-
tradicted their own philosophy supposedly designed to defend the
freedom and dignity of the individual Takuboku felt to be an evasion
of responsibility.

Takuboku's first criticism of Naturalism in "Sporadic Feelings and
Reflections" is directed toward the argument presented by
Hasegawa Tenkei (1876–1940), an outspoken apologist of the
movement. A prolific writer of acute sensibility and forceful style,
Hasegawa had in 1908 alone written three important essays, "Sorrow at the Exposure of Reality," "Solved and Unsolved" and "Various Aspects of Realism," in which he champions Naturalism as the
most down-to-earth literary theory and the one closest to his view of
life. In "Solved and Unsolved," for instance, he argues that the
foundation of human existence rests only in physical reality and that
the candid description of this reality in aesthetic form is art. The
writer's responsibility is therefore not to attempt an interpretation
of life but simply to present his observation of it. Further, it is not
the function of the arts to try to present solutions for human problems; it is a violation of the fundamental principle for the existence
of the arts. Naturalism adapted to this credo of detached observation
as the foundation of its literary viewpoint is not a philosophy of life
but a mere aesthetic theory. Hasegawa therefore believes that distance between literature and life must be maintained if a true
Naturalistic work of art is to be created. It is this emphasis on the
separation of literature from life that Takuboku finds objectionable:

> When Mr. Hasegawa Tenkei once dealt with the question of "the state"
> from the standpoint of Naturalism, he attempted a seemingly innocent
> subterfuge (or so I believe). If, as he says, Naturalism is in no need of ideals
> or solutions, and, since it observes things exactly as they are, it has no
> connection with the existence of the state, its courageous battle against the
> falsity of dated morals ends up a combat in name only. In the observation of
> the world yesterday and today, it is an obvious error to discuss the charac-
> teristics and development of morals while separating moral thought from
> the organism of the state: it is a form of cowardice most particular to the
> Japanese. (IV, 224)

In the last part of the essay Takuboku's argument is directed
toward one of the leading figures of the movement, Tayama Katai

(1871–1930). Katai, along with Shimazaki Tōson, the author of *The Broken Commandment*, had so to speak "naturalized" the Naturalistic movement, giving it a distinctively Japanese coloring. Tōson's work, which Natsume Sōseki praised as the greatest literary achievement of the Meiji era, was the first full-length Naturalistic novel in Japan. It dealt with the problem of discrimination against an outcast group and was the first attempt by any novelist in the Meiji period to commit himself to a social issue. By presenting himself as a voice of conscience, Tōson bridged the gap between life and literature, and his novel was widely acclaimed for its daring content artistically handled. *The Broken Commandment* thus seemed at its appearance in 1906 to have decided the direction of the modern Japanese Naturalistic novel.

However, in the following year, when Katai's *The Quilt* was published, Japanese Naturalism was narrowed. It was Katai's work, not Tōson's, that determined the destiny of the Japanese Naturalistic movement. *The Quilt* is an autobiographical-confessional novel dealing with a writer, married and middleaged, who falls in love with a young woman disciple staying in his home. Caught between his moral obligations as a husband and father and his desire for the young woman, and unable to resolve the dilemma, he suffers continuous frustration. The novel ends with the young woman leaving his house, where the protagonist left alone cries over the quilt on which she had slept.

The ending of the novel is certainly overtly sentimental. However, in spite of its emotionalism and the fact that the work is in literary value inferior to Tōson's *The Broken Commandment*, the novel was enthusiastically received by the critics of the day. Tōson's novel was highly assessed for its well developed subject, whereas Katai's was valued not so much for the content as for the clear demonstration of the author's attitude as a novelist. In other words, it was Katai's calm detachment in the observation of his personal life and his pretenseless realism in the description of his world, both external and internal, that made the critics accept *The Quilt* with enthusiasm. The novel thus marked the beginning of a new era of the Japanese novel. From that time to the present the Japanese Naturalistic novel has been dominated by the realistic autobiographical novel, for which Katai's novel had become the standard form.

In spite of this high appraisal by Katai's contemporaries, however, *The Quilt* contained a serious weakness: it lacked a wider perspective on society. The world outside that of the author's strictly private life was largely ignored; Katai and his followers failed to realize that this concentration on their private worlds was resulting in alienation from life on a larger scale. This paradox Katai did not acknowledge; he gradually grew self-complacent with his kind of literature. In his essay, "How to Write a Novel," in 1909, which Takuboku must surely have read, he further widened the distance between art and life:

Scientists have coolly examined human beings as animals. . . . Religious leaders in their attempts to indoctrinate people as to the nature of faith, ideals and love, have conducted experiment after experiment on man and made his nature clear. The attitude the scientists have maintained has been one of detachment as if the elucidation of truth were their only concern. They have promoted "detached examination" for which we must pay due respect.

The true purpose of the novel is to utilize what science has discovered. It is the function of the novel to describe realistically and in detail "the phenomena" that are the manifestation of the complex psychological activities taking place behind them. Therefore the novelist needs to have more "detachment" than the scientist.[2]

Katai's "scientific" observation, then, means simply an objective analysis and examination of life as well as a candid portrayal of it. He therefore rejects fictionalization of life as long as it is not derived from actual experience or from first hand observation. Yet Katai's reference to "life" needs some qualification: it is confined to *his* life. Therefore his emphasis on exactness in observation and preciseness in expression is the very cause of his separation from life in the larger dimension.

Takuboku's disagreement is with Katai's emphasis on an almost cold impeccability as a professional writer, and his criticism of Katai is focused on this point:

In short, I think that because he deals with life as a "fact to describe," namely he is so passionate in his pride in being a "literary man," he tends to ignore the relationship between human life and himself as a human being. Yes, I am sure there exists that tendency in him. Has his writing not become too professionalized? His style certainly manifests his strong detached realism with the tendency of putting life aside. I am dissatisfied with the way Mr. Tayama always maintains a certain distance between literature and life. He has brought literature close to life and carried it farther away from life at the same time. . . . In that fact I believe lies his cowardice as a man. (IV, 225–26)

For Takuboku literary achievement for its own sake is of no more worth than doodling on scratch paper. He sees that Katai has used literature as a means of escape, evading the most essential issue, namely the writer's place in society. "Sporadic Feelings and Reflections" thus ends with Takuboku's new perspective on the place literature holds in society and his new sense of commitment as a man of letters.

D. *The Birth of a New Idealism*

Takuboku's apprehension concerning the encroachment of the increasing autocratic state, which had begun to exert more restrictions over the individual's freedom, was confirmed sooner than he might have anticipated. In 1910 the High Treason Incident broke out, taking many by surprise. To Takuboku it was a vivid illustration of imperialism undermining the right of the individual to freedom of thought. From this point on the entire political system became to Takuboku an enemy of the people, and he must have been waiting for the opportune moment to voice his opinion on the current national situation. The opportunity presented itself when the August 22, 1910, issue of the *Asahi* published an article in the arts section entitled "Naturalism: The Voice of Individualism" by Uozumi Setsuro. Uozumi was a disciple of Natsume Sōseki, then the editor of the section. The appearance of the essay provided the stimulus Takuboku needed to synthesize his ideas about literature and life, which had so far received only piecemeal expression. The result was "The Present State of the Age of Repression," which he wrote immediately after reading Uozumi's article.

As the subtitle of "The Present State of the Age of Repression," "the fall of authoritarianism and of pure Naturalism and the examination of tomorrow," indicates, the significance of the essay lies in the fact that Takuboku the literary critic and Takuboku the critic of life are combined as one, and for that reason the essay is more than mere literary criticism. The relationship between life and literature is firmly established, and the ambivalence Takuboku held toward Naturalism has completely disappeared as the awareness of the new idealism begins to crystallize his life view. "The Present State of the Age of Repression" is his declaration of intellectual independence of

the Naturalistic movement and affirmation of his faith in the coming
of a new era, a new Japan. It presents a vision of tomorrow to be
realized by the rightful inheritors of today: youth. At first glance the
essay seems to center its argument against Uozumi's interpretation
of the contribution of Naturalism, but Takuboku's principal concern
is to have it serve a corrective purpose. Takuboku takes great pains to
enlighten the readers, particularly the young readers, so that they
may become aware of the predicament in which they are placed and
may learn how to correct it.

Takuboku must have been eager to see his essay published right
away in the *Asahi* as the counter-argument to Uozumi's, but the
piece was turned down. In view of the fact that it was openly critical
of government policies, it is understandable that the *Asahi* rejected
it: the government had begun extensive censorship over all writings
favorable to socialism or critical of the government. Takuboku's essay was published posthumously in 1913.

E.   *Uozumi's "Naturalism: The Voice of Individualism"*

Before we proceed to examine "The Present State of the Age of
Repression" let us study Uozumi's essay so that we can better look at
Takuboku's article in context. Uozumi's "Naturalism: the Voice of
Individualism" is a succinct summary of the characteristics of the
Japanese Naturalistic movement, and the essay, carefully thought
out and substantiated with keen insight, validates Uozumi's own
status as a gifted literary critic. Uozumi maintains that Naturalism is
a dynamic literary movement enabling progressive writers to preserve their individual freedom in their confrontation with authority.
The energy that renders possible their struggle with and survival in
the face of authoritarian power is, Uozumi holds, a unique union of
the two conflicting points of view associated with Naturalism, a
peculiar combination of optimism brought about by emphasis on
self-worth and pessimism stemming from the influence of scientific
determinism, a view imported from the West. The marriage of these
contradictory views has produced the powerful force which has enabled the Naturalists to combat the encroachments of authority:

At the beginning of the modern age [in Europe] the Renaissance and the
Reformation, which were basically incompatible, were once allies to confront their mutual enemy, authority. Likewise [in today's Japan], the realistic and scientific, in other words, the common and fatalistic, viewpoint is

wedded with poignant self-consciousness to expand the self by the power of will. The mysterious union of the two is called Naturalism. They are confronted with a mutual enemy against which they must unite: the power of authority.[3]

In Europe the authority against which the Renaissance and Reformation movements fought was that of the Church, but in Japan the campaign for liberation from the oppression of authority is carried out in a different context. Ultimate authority in Japanese society is represented by three different institutions: 1) the central government (political), 2) Japanese society itself, led and governed by the state (social) and, 3) most uniquely Japanese, the family system (moral and ethical). The tradition surrounding the family is a microcosm of the entire political and social system. The family system, in combination with the two thousand years' tradition of a strong central political authority, has been operating as the primary obstacle to the independence, personal development and expansion of rights of the individual. Uozumi believes that although some Naturalistic writers are simply insensitive to the relationship of literature to the state or the family system, the Naturalists on the whole contributed much to awaken the people to the worth of the individual.

Uozumi's conclusion on the contribution of Naturalism helped Takuboku form his own counter-conclusion. Takuboku readily acknowledged Uozumi's argument as valuable, but at the same time he saw through the flaws in Uozumi's premise that had led to a false conclusion.

F. *"The Present State of the Age of Repression"*

"The Present State of the Age of Repression" is composed of five sections in which Takuboku builds up step by step his powerful argument against current government policies by means of a thorough analysis of the drawbacks of the Naturalists, closing the essay with an affirmation of a new idealism for the future. The opening section of the essay is concerned with Uozumi's argument, particularly with what he missed in his judgment of the contribution of the Naturalistic movement. Takuboku, while acknowledging the essay as invaluable for an understanding of the movement, holds that Uozumi's evaluation of the achievement of the Naturalistic writers is incomplete on grounds that he ignored one undeniable fact. Naturalism from its beginning had contained a serious contradiction because it attempted to combine individualism with scientific determinism. Since then its premise has always been vulnerable. It was really only a matter of time for the flaws of the movement to become apparent. Both Naturalistic and nonNaturalistic writers were fully aware of the contradiction from the start. By disregarding it the Naturalists advertised the movement as if it were founded on unshakable philosophical and aesthetic grounds, and they completely neglected to analyze the nature of the contradiction or attempt a resolution so as to make their basic argument truly unassailable. They devoted their creative energy to the movement without realizing the simple fact that the longer they ignored the inherent contradiction the more the contradiction grew beyond control, until finally it became too large for them even to attempt a solution. As a result what Naturalism advocated pointed in all directions, bringing about confusion not only among readers but among the writers who had placed their faith in the movement. During the past five years, for example, the very definition of Naturalism has been a subject of endless debate without anyone's having ever arrived at a clear idea about it. Takuboku argues that Naturalism for lack of one central idea has become self-defeating and no longer serves any significant purpose either as a philosophical argument or as a literary movement.

Takuboku sees that the two basic and contradictory views of Naturalism, namely, the claim of individualism on the one hand and the negation of the self as defined by scientific determinism on the other, the view commonly called pure Naturalism, are only seemingly in harmony with one another. The truth of the matter is that these two viewpoints are not operating as a combined force to fight against "authority" as Uozumi argues. They are in fact split, each remaining in its own camp. To Takuboku the separation of the two is complete insofar as the pure Naturalists have established what they call *"kanshō-ron,"* or a theory of an objective observation of life as the manifesto of their literary theory. In their view, Takuboku argues, there is no way for the individual to preserve his identity. Their decision to remain onlookers of life thus helped widen the already unbridgeable gap between themselves and the other Naturalists, who claimed the assertion of individualism to be the essence of Naturalism. Takuboku believes in the final analysis that Uozumi has created a false assumption so as to induce the reader to accept his interpretation of the contribution of the Naturalistic movement. As Takuboku sees it, Uozumi's argument is based on the unwarranted assumption that the Naturalists are waging war against an enemy. But the truth of the matter is that the Japanese people, including even the young people, are unaware even of the existence of the enemy:

Our youth in Japan have never come into conflict with authority. Therefore there has existed as yet no opportunity for the state to be our enemy. . . . As far as our problems in relation to the state are concerned (whether they are today's or those of the future of which we are a part), everything is entrusted to the hands of our parents. It is only when the state begins to affect our interests that it enters into our thinking. When it ceases to concern us, the relationship between us and it becomes that of strangers again. (IV, 257–58)

At the end of section one, then, Takuboku carefully shifts from criticism of Uozumi's essay to the discussion of present day youth; in section two he goes on to examine the actual conditions of society and young people's indifference to them. Education, for instance, has become a special privilege of the children of the rich, and only one third of them will be able to continue it because of the ruthless system of entrance examinations. The poor, on the other hand, are suffering from high taxation that restricts the money available for daily food, not to mention the opportunity for education. These very obvious facts, however, apparently fail to stir up the conscience of youth against the government. The youths' lack of concern is due to their preoccupation with their own welfare; they are unaware that by their lukewarm patriotism they are encouraging the prevalence of injustice. Takuboku believes that what they consider good citizenship is nothing more than unconscious subservience to an autocratic state. This submission, or loss of self, has given rise to despair: "They say: 'The country must be strong; we do not have any reasons for opposing the idea. However, we refuse to offer any help' " (IV, 258). Their thinking is to preserve their independence by refusing direct assistance to the government. The so-called "modern individualism," cherished by these youths at the expense of true independence, is then self-deceptive, only reflecting their depression and clearly revealing the fact that the world they live in is moving toward a dead end. The youth are simply incapable of seeing through the reality of things and of taking a more active role in relation to the state as a result of perceiving what it actually is:

Thus it became apparent that what Mr. Uozumi calls the mutual enemy does not in fact exist. Of course, it does not mean that that enemy does not contain the possibility of becoming an enemy; rather it means that we have not made of it our enemy. This union [of contradictory ideas] owes not so much to external reasons as to the fact that from the beginning, when the conflict between these two views was already recognized, till today, neither has had an enemy. (IV, 259)

In the third section Takuboku recapitulates the ideological confusion caused by the Naturalistic writers themselves, this time specifically citing some names. He tries to show the variety of definitions, or one should say, the lack of definition, of Naturalism. Such writers and critics as Tayama Katai, Shimazaki Tōson, Shimamura Hōgetsu (1871–1918), Masamune Hakuchō (1879–1962), Hasegawa Tenkei and Iwano Hōmei (1873–1920) all call themselves Naturalists, but there exists no uniformity in their views of the school to which they belong. The emphasis of the movement constantly shifts, sometimes stressing the deterministic view of life that denies freedom of will, and other times posing as an advocate and protector of individualism. These Naturalistic writers have made no attempt to resolve the contradiction, which has become increasingly obvious to anyone with a perceptive mind.

Naturalism in its present state, Takuboku goes on to argue in the next section, is in no condition to function as a philosophy to imbue youth with hope and a passion for reforming society:

Just as at the time of the rise of Naturalism, even today having no ideal, sense of direction or exit, they [the youth] do not know what to do with their long-accumulated strength. The fact that they are not aware that they have allied themselves with pure Naturalism, which is already extinct, and also the introspective and suicidal tendency among them, clearly show the sad reality that has resulted from the loss of an ideal; this is, in fact, the consequence of "the age of repression." (IV, 261–62)

In a confined world of no exit, one cannot exercise one's imagination so as to grow or let others grow. Take a young aspiring teacher, for example. Knowing that the proper function of education is to create a better future through teaching, he is willing to sacrifice himself to provide children with a good education; nevertheless, the world demands that the children become immediately useful to society, thus contradicting the teacher's ideal. When the pressure of the world is too great, his ideal is inevitably shattered, and "education" becomes merely a means of satisfying the appetite of pragmatic society that discounts the importance of the children's humanity. Consequently, the teacher's energy will be spent in turning out mediocre students, his principles and dreams subsumed in the slogan, "for the sake of society." He must leave the world of education completely if he wishes to try to realize his dreams as a conscientious educator.

Or, Takuboku continues, to look at the other side of the situation, one can easily perceive another obvious consequence of the closed-in society. Many adults say that students have become docile. Yet their apparent docility is nothing but a pretense to cover up worries and anxieties concerning their future. Takuboku knows well that hundreds of graduates of colleges and universities, public and private, are sitting idle, jobless and bored. These former students are even fortunate, in fact, compared with those who were by poverty deprived of the opportunity, if not the right, of receiving higher education. All these phenomena are very obvious effects of the repressive society. The air surrounding the younger generation, which should be vibrant with the promise of the future, is stagnant, and there are ominous signs that confirm the fear that the power of the autocratic state is steadily spreading all over Japan. Takuboku believes that the time has come for the youth to become aware of the presence of the enemy, which has brought their world to stagnation and a dead end, leaving them in despair. It is high time for the youth therefore to assert their worth as human beings. In order to do this: "We must first of all stand up and declare war against the repression of this age. Abandoning Naturalism, . . . we must concentrate our attention on the systematic examination of our own age" (IV, 263).

In the fifth section Takuboku concludes the essay by proposing a positive alternative for securing the place of the individual in the confining society: "An interrogation of tomorrow! This is the only thing we should do today, and all we need to do" (IV, 263). How and in what direction one could best attempt to conduct the investigation Takuboku does not concretely indicate. But he believes that by observing carefully how the recently past younger generation tried to realize the infinite claim of individuality, in short, by learning a lesson from the failures of the experiments performed by Takayama Chogyū, Tsunajima Ryōsen and the Naturalists, today's youth should, he believes, be able to discover an alternative for a better future.

It was Takayama who first tried to comprehensively show by way of Nietzsche's philosophy the worth and potential of the individual. Takayama's interest shifted toward the end of his life to the worship of Nichiren, an uncompromising Buddhist priest and the founder of the Nichiren sect of Buddhism in thirteenth-century Japan. A man of dynamic personality, Nichiren unrelentingly attacked established sects as heretical and criticized rulers patronizing these heretics. For his determination even to sacrifice his life for the cause, he was much admired by his followers; but at the same time he made many enemies. He was eventually exiled for his outspoken censure of both religious and political leaders. In addition to this unyielding singleminded spirit, Nichiren possessed another aspect that captured Takayama's imagination. He had a vision of Japan as "the land in which the true teaching of Buddha was to be revived and from which it was to spread throughout the world."[4] Into this conviction of Nichiren Takayama read a nationalistic bent. It is apparent therefore that Takayama found the most ideal character in the medieval religious leader: the personification of the perfect unity of Nietzschean individualism and nationalistic instinct. The harmony of the two contradictory views is the ultimate goal at which Takayama himself wished to arrive.

Takayama's change of emphasis from Nietzsche to Nichiren Takuboku takes as a clear indication of Takayama's attempt at compromise between Nietzsche's philosophy and the power of organized authority. The compromise, Takuboku maintains, is necessitated by a basic weakness inherent in Takayama's narrow viewpoint. Too much possessed by the naive belief that man's potential is limitless, he had only the most limited comprehension of the power of the socio-political structure and of the position of youth within it: he lacked the insight to recognize the state as the enemy of the people. It was natural, therefore, that youth, "the spirit of the future," had begun to lose interest in Takayama even before he chose Nichiren, a voice from the past, over Nietzsche, "the projector of the future." From Takayama's "experiment" today's youth can learn: "Without changing the present social structure, it is impossible for us to construct within it a new world for ourselves" (IV, 264).

The second noteworthy investigation was a religious one in which the true self was discovered only through its negation: through complete union with the Supreme Being. Tsunajima Ryōsen had published an essay in 1905 in which he described his actual successful attempt at seeing God face to face. Yet the experiment was to Takuboku a failure because the self that found God was one that was ill with tuberculosis, and knowing that the state of spiritual beatitude did nothing to cure the physical disease made Takuboku reluctant to accept Tsunajima's experiment wholeheartedly. Scientific skepticism, said Takuboku, pulls down one's aspiration to fly up to heaven with Tsunajima. Though his account had roused the reader's curiosity, hope and longing, such an experiment is, after all, one in which not all can participate.

The third "experiment" was carried out by the Naturalists, as we have already seen. The result, that is to say the failure, of the experiment has taught a lesson more serious and valuable than the precepts of the first two, namely, that: "Every beautiful ideal is a deception" (IV, 265).

Takuboku therefore concludes the essay: "Thus our direction is almost defined by these three experiments. That is to say, our ideal should no longer be the fantasy of 'good' or 'beauty.' With all fantasies rejected, the only truth left is Necessity! This is the only goal for us to pursue for our future. We must examine 'today' most thoroughly, bravely and freely, in order to discover in it the necessity of our own tomorrow. Necessity is the most real ideal" (IV, 265). In the essay Takuboku has not set forth a clear definition of his conception of "necessity." The term has been interpreted by Marxist critics of Takuboku as "inevitability," but Kunisaki Mokutarō has recently given it a definition that seems to be closer to Takuboku's intention: "Takuboku's conception of Necessity cannot be the objective inevitability observed in existing history which we ourselves actively influence. To listen to his varied human needs, to respond to the demand for total liberation of the ego which speaks from the depth of his heart, or to follow the voice of resistance to that which threatens his existence—all internal, namely subjective, truth is connoted by the word 'Necessity'."[5] In other words, the awareness of "necessity" is born in the mind which remains free and true to what the inner self dictates, the self awakened by the conviction of a new day to come. Takuboku's new idealism is thus founded on full self-knowledge without which one cannot be free in the true sense of the word. The rise of true individualism necessary for the construction of a free society will hasten the fall of the autocratic state. Thus in his essay Takuboku has advanced with persuasive argument a possibility for youth to discover an exit from the closed-in society so that they can build a new world of, by and for their own generation.

"The Present State of the Age of Repression" is a unique essay in that Takuboku has juxtaposed literary criticism with criticism of society so as to give full expression to his literary theory. Through this essay Takuboku put into practice his firm belief that literature and life are inseparable, a conviction which clearly separated him from the Naturalistic writers.

Takuboku was not by any means a systematic thinker; he was rather an essayist driven by strong impulses to express opinions about whatever affected him in some way or another. An individualist, he grew easily enraged at anything that threatened directly or indirectly the freedom of the individual, which he considered indispensable for the development of a truly civilized modern society. Takuboku's prose works are indeed the testimony of his growth not only as a literary critic but as a courageous critic of Japanese society complacent with rapid growth in its political and economic power, both domestic and international. The voices speaking in the essays examined in this chapter, which are the voices of Takuboku's conscience, bespeak his genuine concern with the destiny of his country, and seek to enlighten readers beyond the particularities of time and space. Takuboku was indeed a man of foresight, ahead of his time, whose vision of the future was derived from analytical and sympathetic observation of the present when writing as a critic both of life and literature.

CHAPTER 3

Woodpecker's Songs

TAKUBOKU'S career as a poet in the western style can be divided into three distinct periods, each characterized by the particular movement in which he was absorbed at the time. His early works were modeled after Romantic poetry, the most popular literary movement during those years. When Naturalism replaced Romanticism as his center of interest, his theme and poetic style shifted accordingly. Takuboku did not become a Naturalistic poet as such, but his poetic perception was sharpened by Naturalism's emphasis on the importance of realism in description. In this period his poetry became more down-to-earth with his imagination focused on the details of everyday life, particularly on his struggle to come to terms with it in his private inner world. In the last phase of his life his poems were oriented toward socialism, which Takuboku believed was the most effective way to realize his vision of a better world. In the following pages we will examine Takuboku's development as a poet through a study of selected representative works from each of these three periods.

I   Longing: *Romantic Poems*

The appearance of *Longing* in May, 1905, was a sensational event in Japanese literary circles. It immediately gained a wide and enthusiastic reading public and became a source of inspiration for other aspiring young poets. Readers were amazed at the precocity of the nineteen-year-old poet. It was rare indeed in those days for a young poet to even have a collection of poems published. Takuboku became known all over Japan as a young poetic genius of "the new style."

In spite of the high appraisal of the collection by Takuboku's contemporaries, however, only a select few of the poems in *Longing* are regarded today as having any literary merit. Hackneyed senti-

71

ments, trite imagery and heavy use of poetic diction are flaws immediately apparent to the reader. As a result it is understandable that when critics discuss Takuboku as a poet they tend to ignore *Longing* and concentrate rather on the poems written toward the end of his life. However, while we can understand the general lack of regard for Takuboku's first published work, a study of his development should not entirely set it aside. Moreover, from the point of view of the subjects dealt with, several of the poems deserve more credit than they are usually given. A careful analysis of them will reveal the seriousness of Takuboku's dedication to the cultivation of his poetic gift. To the young aspiring poet, the new movement in poetry held out promise of infinite possibilities, and participation in it was a matter of deep seriousness.

To grasp the essential characteristics of *Longing* it should suffice to examine a few representative poems. For the sake of convenience, let us divide them into two groups, one group to deal with young Takuboku's Romantic view of poetry and the poet, and the second with his meditative poems. Though naively idealistic, Takuboku in his own way tried to come to terms with the nature of poetry, its function in real life, and by using poetry as a vehicle for the contemplation of life, to define his place as a poet.

The first group is represented by such poems as "Reminiscence of the Forest," in which the poet is presented as a healer of human suffering:

> Sing Cuckoo!
> If you and I keep singing to this world
> The everlastingness of spring and spirit,
> The people will be turned from sadness, cleansed.[1]

Or by "Standing on the Tsurukai Bridge" which finds Takuboku presenting his belief that the poet's dwelling place is somewhere beyond the mundane world: "In the palace where light and darkness are made, / Reigns the poet, the sacred lord of the spirit." Further, by "The Ship of Life" which defines poetry as "a ship of life" protected by divine power which directs its way to the gate of paradise, and by "The Echo" in which the poet with a "pure heart" is portrayed as the receiver of a voice from the valley of dreams and the poem as a transmitter of the voice to others. The idea of poetry and the poet expressed in these poems clearly reflects the traditional Romantic view: the poet is a man divinely endowed with a special gift for perceiving and feeling more than do ordinary people, and living only "in the world of solitude, the world of Beauty and the gods" (V, 93). Poetry, "a flower of the ideal, a shadow of a god" (VII, 44), enables one to see the visionary world of beauty and truth. Thus, as the supreme creation of man poetry augments the meaning and beauty of his day-to-day existence.

We can examine this Romantic ideal of poetry more in detail in three other poems: "The Song of a Flower Guardian," "A Woodpecker" and "A Cuckoo." "The Song of a Flower Guardian" is an allegory dealing with the conflict between the poet and the world, and begins with a description of the guardian's strong commitment to his flowers:

> It is daybreak.
> To the call of life
> I open the gate of the garden,
> A mansion in my heart.
> Light, shed thy life on the flowers.
> With a fence built between dreams
> I guard the garden in the solitary land.

Solitary though it is, the garden is full of natural fragrance, music, light, vitality and most important, dreams. Outside the garden is the world of glaring beauty, represented by proud maidens dressed in gold. One bright calm afternoon in the past, the curious guardian, lured by the maidens' beauty, had gone out to "the golden palace of the city" only to find that the world outside was hostile to him:

> The forbidding maidens who guard the gate
> Refused me and said: "Throw away
> The key to the garden."
> Horrified by their hollow smiles,
> Which are animated by the power of the palace,
> I rushed back to my garden.

The guardian is therefore fully satisfied with life inside the garden because free from the threats of the maidens he can enjoy watching his flowers grow upward toward heaven, unaffected and unspoiled

by worldly influence. He takes delight in seeing the flowers move
like big waves, giving him a glimpse of the heavenly home of
dreams. Completely content with his private world of beauty, the
guardian is the self-appointed king of the domain:

> The garden with no night and day
> With the barrier only linking dream with dream
> Hides the key to open the gate of paradise.
>
> Night, come down
> And enwrap all.
> The gate of the garden
> Stands unaffected by the eternal darkness.
> Of my garden in the solitary land
> With the fountain of light,
> Shining it on the world,
> I am the king.

The allegorical meaning of the poem is obvious: the garden of
flowers is poetry and the guardian is the poet himself. The function
of the poet, then, as Takuboku sees it, is to separate himself from
the world that fails to understand his mission, and to live in his own
sheltered world of poetry. He knows that only in the world of beauty
and dreams can he find full satisfaction and happiness. Not yet
burdened with family obligations and not yet faced with the discrepancy between real life and the world of his imagination, young
Takuboku can indulge in complacent posturing as a godlike figure
who dwells apart. "The Song of a Flower Guardian" has little literary value; the subject is trite and the images are commonplace. But
despite these obvious flaws the poem does reveal Takuboku's sincere dedication to poetic composition, a sincerity which salvages an
otherwise superficial piece.

The idealized Romantic view of poetry and the poet is further
illustrated in "A Woodpecker," modeled after a western sonnet:

> In the green forest, the Spirit's habitat,
> Echoes the immortal sound of the bell of Love,
> Forged in the eternal fire of Heaven,
> And struck by the saints in the forest of Athens.
> Listen! a woodpecker's pecking all day long,
> Warning against the encroaching of the dust storm
> About to assault the sacred forest of the Spirit,

Which is filled with youthful life.
Three thousand years have passed and years are still passing.
But how immortal Plato's teaching is!
It reaches beyond the swift arrow of Time,
Flies beyond the trace of the formless white arrow.
Guarding the glory of Plato's ideals,
The small bird performs his inspired mission.

"The dust storm" is Takuboku's favorite image for the arid life of the city where humanity is dried up.[2] Juxtaposing a forest, or nature, with city life is a characteristically Romantic approach. The forest is a source of inspiration for the poet, whose concern is with the preservation of purity, beauty and good. It is his responsibility to warn society against losing these values, no matter how futile his efforts may seem. Poetic creation is then the poet's means of expressing serious commitment to his ideals; and the role of the poet, as is made clear by linking his message with the teachings of the philosopher, is that of a prophet recalling man to the virtues that preserve the true meaning of his life.

In "A Cuckoo" Takuboku is concerned with the function of imagination. The poem is composed of six stanzas all together, and in the third and fourth stanzas Takuboku sings:

In my childhood, too, in the green field
I heard the voice; I again hear it here.
As a poet's thought lives on forever,
The bird's voice appears to have eternal life, too.

Eternity! an immortal twinkling of an eye.
Twinkling of an eye! Short-lived eternity in a moment.
My life and my poem (which have momentary permanence)
They may fade away, as the voice has disappeared,
Yet though they die away, their death is
    an immortal twinkling.
Even if this world should come to an end,
I wish to live on as the voice lives on.

The poem has a striking similarity to Wordsworth's "To the Cuckoo," which treats the redemptive power of imagination. Like Wordsworth Takuboku believes that the creative imagination enables the poet to see into the pattern of permanence in the world of change and decay and to sustain it through poetic creation. The voice of the cuckoo Takuboku listens to is, of course, not the same one he heard in his childhood. Through the enactment of a past experience in the present, however, the imagination enables the poet to perceive in it a sustained image of immortality. The moment vitalized by the imagination is the immortal moment of awareness because the poet is able to probe into the nature of human experience: an intense moment of beauty is enriched by the memory of a former similar experience, and the moment fully lived gives the poet a sense of fulfillment. The poem is then the record of an invaluable moment captured by the creative imagination and a means of preserving the immortal quality inherent in transient human experience. The poet sees the possibility of a rich and intense life and, by expressing this poetically, gives hope for a new life, an eternal life, as is shown at the close of the poem: "My life and my poem are the symbol of eternity:/ Thus I will sing, as my bird-friend does,/ To participate in the march of infinite Life."

Takuboku's view of poetry is certainly idealistic, so idealistic in fact that his poems treating the subject are contrived and superficial. Yet his concern with imagination and stress on poetry is part of his overall philosophy of life. His poetic creation represented his individual effort to preserve human values in the rapidly changing society of the Meiji era. Takuboku's idealized view of the poet, nourished through his apprenticeship in Romanticism, was to harden into a conviction sustaining his commitment to a life of letters.

II   Longing: *Poems of Meditation*

Being the son of a Zen priest, it is not surprising that Takuboku wrote poems of meditation on Buddhist themes. Such poems as "The Hidden Marsh," "On a Fallen Roof-tile," "The Bell at Twilight," "The Evening Bell," "The Shadow of a Tower" and "The Moon and the Bell" show his thorough assimilation of the Buddhist teaching which stresses the transitoriness of human life and the futility of human achievement. Takuboku's employment of the Buddhist terms associated with the conditions of man's existence in the world of change and decay give the poems an added richness.

The poems range in content from religious contemplation on the human condition to aesthetic description of the nature of solitude. Of the religio-contemplative poems cited above, the most representative is "On a Fallen Roof-tile." The poem is undoubtedly modeled after Susukida's "To a Broken Pot," the best of the Symbolist's early poems. Before we go on to a discussion of Takuboku's poem, it will be useful to contrast the two poets' treatments of a similar subject.

At the sight of the broken pieces of pot lying on the earthen floor of a farmer's kitchen, the poet is seized by melancholy as he becomes aware of the mortality of all things including himself:

> The pure is fragile,
> So sing the poets.
> The good must be brittle, too,
> The old water pot is smashed.
>
> Man born of clay,
> He who traces the pure way,
> He who longs for heaven,
> His destiny is like the pot's.
>
> The old pot is crushed.
> Sorrow-stricken,
> I stand on the broken pieces,
> Not knowing the sun has set.

Everything that man cherishes is destined to pass away. This is the predicament he must face in his mortal existence. For Susukida this painful awareness is in fact the dilemma and paradox every artist has to confront: the artist's creative imagination, though immortal in itself, is destined to fall a prey to the force of time once it is embodied in a material object of art, which by nature is doomed to decay. Artistic creation is thus at once both a blessing and a curse: a blessing because it beautifies the world of mortality; a curse because the created object is vulnerable to the encroachment of time.

In a similar fashion, in his poem "On a Fallen Roof-tile" Takuboku uses a ruined object as a starting point for meditation on human experience. To the poet the fallen tile is a symbol of the impermanence of all things, not only of works of art but also of man's glory and dreams:

> The faint sound of a bell lingers
> In the grass-covered garden
> At autumn even-fall.

> A decayed roof-tile covered with faded moss,
> Carved with the names of old believers,
> Has fallen and shattered
> Sadly telling the ruins of dreams
> Of the long gone past.

Takuboku's concern, therefore, like Susukida's, is with the impact of time on all aspects of human life. Yet there is a marked contrast between the two poets in their treatment of the subject. With simple language and style Susukida has successfully created the intense feeling of pathos coming from his realization of transience, a realization that nullifies even the artist's aspirations to create. The intensity Susukida feels is that of the artist compelled to accept this irreconcilable fact of life. Takuboku, on the other hand, is more concerned with creating the tone of melancholy sadness that arises from the awareness that he as a man is not freed from death:

> How similar my destiny to that of the fallen tile!
> . . . .
> Like a string of the zither
> I am merely a sparkle of light
> That brightens a string of life longing for eternity
> Dimly burning in a space between dark and confusion.
> On the day the string breaks,
> I will die, though I know not the place;
> Like an arrow gone wide of the mark,
> Flying with a faint whiz
> Only to fall to decay in the high grass.

In the above passage, through effective use of simile Takuboku has succeeded in producing a certain meditative poetic atmosphere; yet in other passages too much dependence on realism in description has made the poem little more than a mere sketch of a temple:

> The pity of it, burning incense with the fragrance
> Of the white orchid in the deep valley.
> The priests with their purple robes swaying,
> The mellow tones of the solemnly-sounding gong
> Sink into the heart.
> In the golden-dragon flames of the well-ordered candles
> Flickers the pillar of Paradise.

Now again evening after evening
The sandlewood smoke,
Within the mother-of-pearl walls of the sanctuary,
Breathes out a rainbow.
Led by the incantation of the chief priest,
His spotless garments loosely belted,
His merciful eyes moist with tears,
Sit the large company of pilgrims old and young.
The hems of their garments in one line,
Among them also a child
Offering up incense and flowers.

Takuboku's contemplation is more that of a Buddhist thinker than an
artist. Detailed description of the temple, the pilgrims visiting it,
the robes of the priests and the fragrance of incense, all assist the
reader to capture the setting. But the poet's effort to create a contemplative mood through graphic description of a particular setting
has led to monotony of style and shallowness in the description of his
own inner feelings. Takuboku has allowed his intellectual grasp of
Buddhist teaching to take precedence over use of his imagination in
his effort to create a work of art. As a result, the language of the
poem, not accompanied by genuine feeling, therefore lacks the intensity the subject calls for—or the tightly knit unity which
Susukida's poem has.

Takuboku's poetic imagination flows more freely when he deals
with the nature of loneliness, as in "The Solitary House." While the
subject is conventional, Takuboku's handling of it is his own. Traditionally, as represented by the poet Bashō (1644–1694), the idea of
loneliness had been associated with loneliness in nature, which
concept in turn had been often used as a metaphor for the loneliness
present in the poet's consciousness. To this conventional treatment
of the subject Takuboku has added a new dimension: the loneliness
of alienation arising from a consciousness of separation from the
world outside:

Angry at the storm of the murky world
I flee into a solitary house at the dreary seashore.
The ancient wave, rolling in and out, crashes
To the sad music of nature the ocean plays.
My lonely body and the heart wander
In silent contemplation.

Having had no shore before,
Where should I steer my soul's solitary ship,
In the aimless journey of life?

The evening tide, the roaring of the bottomless heart,
Its color and sound, all in eternal harmony,
This instant at sunset, languidly rolls in and is smashed—
The setting sun gazes on me, and I at the sun, shouting:
"Infinite Darkness or Light without end, bury all."

The poet's anxiety stems from his feeling of isolation from society, originating in his own selfconsciousness. Examined in the light of the intellectual trend of the time, when young thinkers were preoccupied with the concept of individualism, the poet demonstrates the destiny of the modern intellectual driven to isolation by his quest for his own identity. The sense of uncertainty brought about by the poet's alienation therefore creates an ambivalence in his attitude toward his own life. His simultaneously invoking "Infinite Darkness" and "Light without end" reveals this ambivalence: on the one hand he is frightened at the uneasiness which will result from his lonely existence; on the other, his independent spirit is exhilarated by the rich prospects life offers him. Takuboku's ambivalence remains unresolved; yet one can see that he recognized that self-awareness and an independent mind were to be purchased only at the price of loneliness and alienation. Takuboku's insight anticipates that of Natsume Sōseki, whose works such as *The Wayfarer* (1912) and *Kokoro* (1914) deal with the impact on the individual's mind of alienation brought on by excessive self-examination. It is noteworthy that Takuboku had already made an estimate of the price one must pay for introspection, a concomitant of the individualism that was to become one of the major themes of modern literature.

Solitude is given more positive treatment in "To Solitude," one of the longest poems in *Longing* and the best meditative poem in the collection. In it Takuboku presents an extensive analysis of the nature of solitude. Like Milton's "Il Penseroso," "To Solitude" is the poet's apostrophe to a solitude which provides him with aesthetic pleasure. There is no evidence that Takuboku had read Milton's poem, yet, if he had not read it, the similarity between "Il Penseroso" and "To Solitude" is a strange coincidence. Rather than Milton's poem the source of inspiration for "To Solitude" is more likely to have been Byron's *Childe Harold's Pilgrim-*

age. In his diary of November 14, 1902, Takuboku remarked on his reading of Canto IV, stanza 178, a stanza he calls "Solitude." Of works he had read in English the stanza was one of his favorites: "There is a pleasure in the pathless woods,/ There is a rapture on the lonely shore,/ There is society, where none intrudes,/ By the deep Sea, and music in its roar:/ I love not Man the less, but Nature more,/ From these our interviews, in which I steal/ From all I may be, or have been before,/ To mingle with the Universe, and feel/ What I can ne'er express, yet cannot all conceal." Byron, along with Napoleon, was to the young Takuboku a personage of great admiration. In his novels, especially *Clouds Are Geniuses*, we can catch a glimpse of the writer in his attempted imitation of his hero setting himself apart from the world in a lofty detachment.

"To Solitude" opens with a description of a tranquil scene: the poet is reading a book alone in his room into which the moon, through a broken window, casts its gentle light. From the garden sounds the chirping of insects replaying the thousand-year-old "sad music of humanity," to use Wordsworth's famous phrase. Solitude, coming into the room with the moonlight, greets the poet. Pleased with her visit, the poet begins to address Solitude, telling her of the many pleasures she offers him.

Like a beloved wife, gentle Solitude is a fitting companion for the meditative poet: "Through the window you silently slide in,/ In the gray clothes of the moonlit shade./ Kindly like a long-awaited wife,/ Smiling, you sit down beside me."

Solitude enables the poet to find peace of mind and freedom from worldly cares: "Behold! Where you quietly breathe,/ The mist of my heart is cleansed./ I see my true self,/ Unmoved by the things around me,/ Dwelling in light./ Where your pulses beat,/ All other noises are silent./ I only hear the echo of billows rolling in,/ In the vast ocean of the heart." This idea is developed further:

> The lovely name, Solitude!
> You are as it were a mirror of secrecy.
> Should a man reflect himself in it,
> His disguises all evaporate
> As a wet leaf quickly dries in the sun,
> Leaving the two complete shadows on its face:
> The naked self with no adornment;
> And the gate that burns with fires of life,

> With the immortal power
> Of great Nature surrounding the self.
> Thus when man speaks to Solitude,
> He speaks of Truth in the words of the self,
> In the voice of his true self.

Takuboku is reiterating the view set forth in "A Woodpecker" and "A Cuckoo," the view that a return to a natural environment restores man to his true self. The poet feels that he can discover his true identity only in withdrawal from human society. His relation with Solitude, then, is a mystic one through which the integrity of his inner self is maintained. With a quasi divine power Solitude leads the poet to self-knowledge and humility:

> The power that compels a head
> Down before the revelation of solemn Heaven—
> That power you possess in your sway.

Finally, and of supreme importance to the poet, Solitude offers him the gratification of heightened poetic inspiration, the visionary experience in which he can commune with the Supreme Being governing both man and nature:

> Ah, Solitude! Where your pulses beat,
> The place where I commune with my Self,
> Inside the multifold fences surrounded by the spirits,
> Lies the beloved garden of flowers of poetry.
> There my soul wanders in quietude.
> All the spontaneous mutterings
> Are prayers dedicated to the god,
> Who rules both man and nature
> Beyond history, decrees and laws of man.

Considering all the satisfactions Solitude affords, the poet realizes that the secular world has nothing comparable to offer:

> When I meet a true man embraced
> In the arms of lovely Solitude as I was,
> Who knows the pleasure of longing in tears
> Beyond time and space,
> I will melt into this moonlight and ask him:
> "How worthy in truth is the land
> That glitters with glory and gold?"

Despite an occasional exaggerated line or trite image, "To Solitude" is a poem satisfactorily handled for an eighteen-year-old youth. Takuboku's treating solitude as a poetic subject, his use of solitude for its own sake rather than as a metaphor for something else, has brought a freshness to the poem. Takuboku sustains the contemplative tone by using throughout a regular metric pattern of 7-4-5; when he does not use this pattern, a variation of it such as 4-7-5 is adopted. He also makes use of a refrain for controlling the meditative mood: "The lovely name, Solitude."

From an artistic point of view the distinguishing characteristic of "To Solitude" is Takuboku's use of simile. To give only a few examples: the moonlight comes in "like an old nun"; the piled up books surrounding the poet are "like the spirit of secrecy/ Sneaking out from its cave in a forlorn valley"; the visit of Solitude is always gentle and swift "like the wind"; the solemnity of Solitude's smile is "like the dark silent forest/ Guarded with hundreds of drawn swords"; when reflected in the mirror of Solitude, all "disguises evaporate/ As a wet leaf quickly dries in the sun." All these similes composed of concrete sensory images add an extra dimension to the poem. Takuboku's apprenticeship in simile, further developed in his tanka, thus began in his writing of poems in the new style.

Not all the meditative poems are religious or philosophical speculations on man and art. "The Sleeping City" is a meditation on city life, one of Takuboku's frequent concerns in earlier stages of his literary development. In this poem Takuboku treats the evils of urban life. Unlike those examined above, this poem is written in simple language devoid of poetic diction. In tone it is more realistic than Romantic, which sets it apart from the majority of the other poems in *Longing* and anticipates Takuboku's later poems employing Naturalistic objectivity in description.

The poem opens with a sketch of a city by night:

> The solemn bell tolls.
> The night is heavy.
> Seen from above,
> The capital with the voices asleep,
> Lies like a dead lion in the wilderness.

The reader is told immediately that the surface serenity of the city is an illusion. The slumber of the city lying "like a dead lion in the wilderness" is the sleep of death. The tolling of a bell and the heaviness of the night intensify the funereal atmosphere. In several other works Takuboku has used a skeleton image to represent city life; a death image, then, is the sustained image in his early writings for describing the effect of city life upon its inhabitants. Death imagery in "The Sleeping City" is further developed in stanzas 2, 3 and 4:

> The restless billows of the fog,
> Frozen in the shadow of gray moonlight,
> Enwrap the whole city.
> Like the shadows of a hundred ships in port,
> The shadow of a lamp is cast.

> Seen from above,
> The sleeping city—
> Is this the castle
> In the sea of blood
> Anticipatory of the last day?
> The evening fog is like a tombstone,
> And buries all living things.

> A million wearied souls
> Appear asleep—in the grave.
> The fog separates earth from heaven
> And the moonlight cannot penetrate
> The heavenly dreamland.

Further, the discrepancy between appearance and reality creates an irony with a chilling effect. The night's sleep is not a state of rest but a process in which the sleepers are stripped of the flesh of humanity, leaving only skeletons. The poet hears the voice of their restless agony, helpless before the all-engulfing torrent of city life:

> In the voiceless city
> Echoes a solemn silent sound,
> Which hangs in the fog and grows louder
> With the roar of the black current.

Contrasted to the city of horror is the poet's room:

> My window
> Like a castle surrounded
> By the turbulent sea,

> Lets in moonlight to every corner
> And protects the heart of poetry
> Frightened at the waves encroaching from afar.

The moonlight reveals the true nature of life beneath the deceptive peaceful sleep of the city. Wakened to awareness by the moonlight, the poet weaves into his poems his new realization. Standing aloof from the world as an observer of it, the poet is better able to see into the nature of city life and through his poetry make his readers more conscious of it. At this point the Romantic ideal of the poet committing himself to the concerns of the common man is brought to the forefront. Takuboku's poetic endeavor to investigate daily human experience anticipates the attitude revealed in the series of poems titled "A Study of the Heart" and those of socialistic sentiment composed toward the end of his life.

The poems in *Longing* are by no means great works. They give the current reader little pleasure and therefore can hardly lure him to return for a second reading. The subject matter is commonplace, conventional poetic diction has been used to excess and the style on the whole is affected and exaggerated. These poems lack the simplicity of style and language that was to become the unique characteristic of Takuboku's later poems, particularly his tanka.

However, as the first major work of Takuboku, compiled in his late teens, *Longing* holds a significant place in his literary career. First of all, the enthusiastic reception the volume received had a tremendous impact on the young poet. That a large number of people enjoyed reading *Longing* clearly indicates the extraordinary gift of the fledgling writer. Takuboku's self-confidence as a poet was abundantly insured by this reception. Secondly, written at a time when Takuboku was free from family obligations, the poems in *Longing* display Takuboku's free play in various types of poetry. He gave unrestrained vent to his imagination in a wide range of experimentation with poetic forms: sonnet, narrative, dirge and visionary poem. His facility in composition gave rise to a self-assurance bordering on arrogance that was doomed to be crushed when he naively assumed that he could with equal ease write novels, a subject to be discussed in the next chapter.

Thirdly, the poems in *Longing* reveal Takuboku's quick adaptability to a literary movement, an innate capacity that manifested itself throughout his career. He possessed a special ability to see through to the essential characteristics of any movement, and he attempted to express his perceptions in various literary forms. When the wave of Romanticism subsided and Naturalism became the prominent movement, Takuboku transferred his interest to the latter at once. His readiness to experiment with whatever new ideas or forms of literary expression came to the shore of Japan led him to try his hand at nearly every genre except drama. Considering the fact that the duration of his creative career was no more than five or six years, it is remarkable that he produced so many works in so short a period.

III *After* Longing

Takuboku continued to write poems even after he began to devote his energies to novel writing. His experimentation with the Naturalistic novel helped him outgrow the Romantic sentimentalism which was apparent in *Longing*. Within two years after the publication of *Longing*, Takuboku's poetic sensibility had changed drastically, as he himself realized. In his essay, "From Yumi-chō: Poems to Eat," he analyzes his early attitude:

After turning seventeen or eighteen I tried my hand at verse-writing for two or three years. In those days poetry was all I had. Only by making poems could I find a way to express the longing for an undefinable something which possessed me. My passion was for nothing but poetry. As everyone knows now, except for fantasy, childish rhythms and a faint element of religion (or of something like it), the poems of those days contained merely hackneyed sentiments. In reflecting on the poetic attitude I had then, I can point out one thing; that is, I certainly went through a troublesome process. For example, suppose I got some feelings from a six-foot tall tree standing in a small vacant lot with the sun shining on it. Unless my imagination changed the open space into a wild plain, the small tree into a giant tree, the sun into the morning sun or the setting sun; not only that, unless I transformed myself, who had been observing all this, into a poet or a traveler, or into a young man of sorrow, it did not seem that the feeling was compatible with the poetic sensibility of the day, and I myself could not be satisfied. (IV, 207–8)

As he gained wider experience of life, Takuboku began more and more to derive the subject matter of his poems from deep levels of daily emotional experience. He began to deal with down-to-earth subjects in accordance with his new view of poetry, again set forth in "From Yumi-chō." Poems, Takuboku pronounces, must be "poems to eat"; that is, poems which truly speak to the human heart are "poems written with both feet firmly on the ground, poems with feelings not divorced from real life. They are neither delicacies nor a feast but our ordinary daily meal: poems that are our necessities" (IV, 212). The poet who creates this kind of poetry is required to have one very basic qualification:

To put it briefly, I deny the existence of a special human being called a poet. It is reasonable for others to call him who makes poems a poet, but the versifier cannot regard himself as such. It may be improper of me to say so, but the fact is that by considering himself to be a poet he is degrading his poetry. . . . To be a poet, one needs three qualifications: first, second and last, to be a human being. He must also be a person who possesses all the qualities that an ordinary man has. (IV. 213–14)

For this sort of poet to express the felt experience of daily life colloquial language and a simple style must be used. This is the one distinguishing conclusion Takuboku had in 1909 arrived at. His poems written during and after that year come close to being what he called "poems to eat."

IV *"A Study of the Heart"*

A group of poems published in the *Mainichi* newspaper in 1909 under the title of "A Study of the Heart"—a peculiarly prosaic title for poems indeed—illustrates the change in Takuboku's poetic sensibility. The set is comprised of five poems, each having its own title: "The Horror of a Town in Summer," "Don't Wake Up!" "A Spring Twilight When Something Is About to Happen," "A Willow Leaf" and "The Fist." Since all these poems are rather short, let us examine each of them to see the new development in Takuboku's poetic perception.

"The Horror of a Town in Summer" reads as follows:

> Under the burning sun of the summer
> The rail of the heart glitters in horror.
> Sliding down from the knees of his sleeping mother,
> A fat little boy three years or so,
> Toddles toward the streetcar rail.
>
> Withered vegetables are at the grocery store.
> The blinds of the hospital windows hang motionless.

Under the closed iron gate of the kindergarten,
A white dog with long ears lies flat.
All in the midst of infinite brightness,
Somewhere a poppy flower has dropped dead,
The gloom of the summer air cracks the green-wood coffin.

An ice-maker's sick wife with a wooden box in hand
Goes out with a broken umbrella spread.
Out of the lodging house at an alley approaches
The funeral procession of a beriberi patient,

Silent to the horror of summer.
Glancing at it, the police
At the street corner stifles a yawn.
The white dog stretched to his content,
Rises and goes to a patch of shade in the dumping ground.

Under the burning sun of the summer
The rail of the heart glitters in horror.
Sliding down from the knees of his sleeping mother,
A fat little boy three years or so,
Toddles toward the streetcar rail.

All images except "the rail of the heart" in the first and last stanzas
are concrete, taken from the familiar world of daily life. In these
common scenes Takuboku describes objectively a drama of life and
death taking place beneath the heat of summer. By using these
scenes almost in an impressionistic manner, he has succeeded in
creating the feeling of the deathlike lethargy of the season, thus
exposing its true nature, paradoxically obscured by the brightness.
    At first glance the opening stanza and the closing stanza—a re-
petition of the opening—do not seem related to the rest of the
poem. They are, in fact, the larger frame of the poem. The tone of
these stanzas determines the mood of the whole poem: terror
created by the awareness of death lying just underneath the glaring
surface. The image of the little boy toddling along toward the streetcar rails heightens the tension of the scene. Because his fate is left
ambiguous, the feeling of uncertain dread is intensified.
    In "The Horror of a Town in Summer" Takuboku concentrated on
creating a certain mood of the summer season; in "A Spring Twilight
When Something Is About to Happen" he evokes the feeling of
uncertainty contained in spring:

War breaks out in a far-away country . . .
At sea a banquet on the wrecked ship . . .

A pale woman stands at a pawn shop
And turns away from the light to blow her nose.
Leaving there, she sees in an alley
A short prostitute patting her lover on the back—
The woman opens her purse under the dim light.

Something is about to happen—
The town at the spring dusk is oppressed
By the heavy murky air of uncertainty.
The long restless day is over,
Wearied, not knowing why.

Many are killed in the far-away country . . .
Women demonstrators shout at the government office . . .
At sea, plagues of the albatross . . .

A lamp falls at a carpenter's.
The wife jumps up!

By juxtaposing a war in a distant place with a day-to-day existence of the people in his immediate neighborhood, the poet tries to show that human misery is universal. While many lives are lost in a war torn land, people in a country at peace suffer from a similar uncertainty of life intensified by poverty. Spring, the season of hope and new life, is also the season of anxiety. There is a faint tone of impending disaster. The effect created by the poem is, however, spoiled by the final two lines. They appear to be an afterthought, stuck on to the poem in order to satisfy the reader's expectations, bearing no organic relation to the poem as a whole. This confusing ending of the poem suggests that Takuboku did not have a clear idea as to what he wanted to say. In spite of the poet's success in evoking a mood, the poem leaves us with the impression that it is contrived.

In the remaining three poems of "A Study of the Heart" Takuboku, dealing with more personal subjects, handles them more effectively. "Don't Wake Up!", for instance, shows us Takuboku's sensitive sympathetic imagination:

There is a life more hollow
Than a dust-filled window,
Heated by the setting sun.

> Utterly wearied from thinking,
> A sweating young man naps snoring,
> Exposing the yellow teeth in his mouth.
> The summer sunlight through the window
> Shines on his hairy shanks
> On which the fleas crawl up.
> Don't wake up; sleep till the sun sets,
> Until the cool and quiet evening comes to your life.
> Somewhere is heard a girl's bewitching laughter.

In his seemingly noncommittal description of the man in sleep, Takuboku reveals a sympathy with the loneliness and isolation of the man who has found in sleeping a momentary oblivion from the misery of life. The poet's compassion for the man is clearly shown by the lines, "Don't wake up; sleep till the sun sets,/ Until the cool and quiet evening comes to your life." These lines are the expression of the poet's genuine wish for the man to continue to sleep even a minute longer, even, perhaps, until death. Takuboku's urging comes from his own feeling that the world of wakefulness is a place of wretchedness from which only sleep gives relief.

At the same time, however, Takuboku knows that the kind of ease one gets from sleep and the poet's own wish to let the man enjoy his peaceful slumber as long as possible are both, after all, deceptions. The world remains cold to those who can find no place in it. It is into this world that the man must sooner or later wake up. Kunisaki maintains that the last line of the poem ("Somewhere is heard a girl's bewitching laughter") is a "voice of life in the midst of an atmosphere of death,"[3] but it could perhaps be better interpreted as a voice of indifference to human loneliness and hopelessness. "Don't Wake Up!" is a poem in which Takuboku has sung with tenderness his own dilemma.

Takuboku's personal response to the pathos of life is further illustrated in "A Willow Leaf":

> Flying in through the streetcar window
> A willow leaf lands on her knees—
>
> Vicissitude is felt here, too.
> This woman also
> Has walked the course of her life.

> With a suitcase on her knees
> This thin, sad-looking yet attractive woman
> Next to me falls asleep.
> Where are you heading?

While the mood and point of view of the poem is identical with that of "Don't Wake Up!" (the poet is again a sympathetic observer of another individual), the setting of "A Willow Leaf" gives the poem an additional dimension. The woman in the train is a traveler, and a journey is of course an image traditionally associated with life itself. Combined with the image of the willow leaf, the journey image thus recreates the sense of pathos felt by the poet. It is obvious that the poet is identifying himself with the woman. He sees her as a lonely traveler like himself, journeying through life with no specific destination. In the imagination of the poet, the woman, the poet himself and the willow leaf are the same. The question "Where are you heading?" directed apparently toward the woman is in fact a question addressed to the willow leaf and to the poet himself. The poet, the woman and the leaf, acted upon by mysterious forces of life, are led each to his own separate destiny. The message of the second stanza is too explicit and even a little didactic, but on the whole, the melancholy sadness that comes from an awareness of the uncertainty of human existence is successfully brought out in the poem.

In the last poem of the group, "The Fist," the subject Takuboku deals with becomes most personal:

> When pitied by a friend richer than I,
> Mocked by a friend stronger than I,
> In rage I lift a fist.
> I then find that anger has withdrawn
> And quiet like a criminal,
> Is crouching with his eyes wide open
> At one corner of the heart.
> Helpless.
>
> How futile it all is!
>
> You don't know what to do with your fist.
> Whom do you intend to strike!
> A friend . . . ? yourself . . . ?
> Or the innocent pillar beside you?

This poem is of course much longer than a tanka, yet the intensity of the poem, condensed to a vivid simile and image, parallels the force that Takuboku demonstrates in his tanka. In simple language Takuboku has brought forth with spontaneity his frustration at being in a condition of poverty, a feeling intensified by the awareness that he is unable to free himself from privation.

In spite of a few obvious drawbacks as poetry, the group of poems in "A Study of the Heart" reveals distinct poetic development. Takuboku's concentration on concrete daily events in his external and inner world has changed his poetic style and language, and images have naturally become more definite and personalized. His imagination no longer directed toward the world of Romantic idealism or sentimentalism, Takuboku has liberated himself from the burden of poetic diction, affectation and the wild fantasy that set his poetry in opposition to his personal life. Combined with realism and the poet's honesty to his inner feelings, "A Study of the Heart" is pointed toward what Takuboku has called "poems to eat," his new ideal of poetry. Takuboku's pursuit of this new poetic ideal was soon accompanied by pursuit of a new society, for whose sake he decided, at least in his rational thinking, to commit himself, to socialism. The poetic works born of this passion for social ideals are the series of poems posthumously published as *Power and Poetry*.

V   Power and Poetry

When the series was published in 1913, there were eight poems, each having its own separate title: "After Endless Discussions," written on June 15, 1911, "A Spoonful of Cocoa," June 15, 1911, "Heated Argument," June 16, 1911, "An Afternoon in My Study," June 15, 1911, "The Epitaph," June 16, 1911, "On Opening a Wornout Bag," June 16, 1911, "A House," June 25, 1911, and "An Airplane," June 27, 1911. But the way Takuboku arranged the series originally was slightly different. There were at first nine poems, written between June 15 and 17, 1911, of which he selected six to be published in *Creative Writing* under the single title "After Endless Discussions" in July, 1911. Toward the end of June, 1911, however, Takuboku became interested in having a second collection of poems published in which he wanted to include some of the verses from the series. After carefully revising the six poems published in *Crea-*

tive Writing (the first six referred to above), he put a title to each of them. He then added two new poems, the last two cited above, which is why the last two are dated later than the other poems.

Concerning the significance of the series for the history of modern Japanese literature, Iwaki has this to say:

Takuboku's *Power and Poetry* was compiled after the High Treason Incident, namely during "the ten years' winter" of socialism. Its particular significance in terms of the history of modern literature lies in that while trying earnestly to keep his feelings attuned to the direction of the age, Takuboku boldly wrote about matters which his contemporaries had deliberately avoided.[4]

Further, Iwaki holds that Takuboku used this series to put forward a strong protest against the injustices of society, a protest raised to the level of longing for a revolution.[5] It is indeed praiseworthy that Takuboku had the courage to call for a socialistic revolution before the tension of the High Treason Incident had yet subsided. However, while agreeing with Iwaki on the historical significance of *Power and Poetry*, examined as poetry, the poems in the collection reveal along with a new poetic achievement some defects that cannot be ignored. In the following pages we shall look at four of the poems which illustrate both the strength and the weaknesses of the series: "After Endless Discussions," "A Spoonful of Cocoa," "An Afternoon in My Study" and "An Airplane."

"After Endless Discussions" reads:

> Our reading and debate and our glittering eyes
> Are no less intense than the Russian youth's fifty years ago.
> We have discussed what we should do
> But no one strikes the table with a clenched fist
> And shouts: "For the people!"
>
> We know what it is we seek,
> What the multitudes desire,
> And what we should do.
> More we know than the Russian youth fifty years ago.
> But no one strikes the table with a clenched fist
> And shouts: "For the people!"

Everyone gathered here is young,
The young who always create the new world.
We know the old die soon and we will finally win.
Look at our glittering eyes and the intense debate.
But no one stikes the table with a clenched fist
And shouts: "For the people!"

Thrice already have the candles been replaced,
The corpse of a small insect floats in a drinking cup.
Though the young woman's zeal is no less than before,
Her eyes reflect the fatigue following endless discussion.
Yet no one strikes the table with a clenched fist
And shouts: "For the people!"

Takuboku took the title from *Memoirs of a Revolutionist* by Peter
Alexeievich Kropotkin, a book he had read just before writing the
poem. The image of "the Russian youth fifty years ago" is derived
from a passage of the book which Takuboku inserted at the end of
"V'Narod Series," a record of Kōtoku's testimony he clandestinely
copied:

In every town of Russia, in every quarter of St. Petersburg, small groups
were formed for self-improvement and self-education; the works of the
philosophers, the writings of the economists, the researches of the young
Russian historical school, were carefully read in these circles, and the
reading was followed by endless discussions. The aim of all that reading and
discussion was to solve the great question which rose before them: In what
way could they be useful to the masses? Gradually, they came to the idea
that the only way was to settle amongst the people and to live the people's
life. Young men went into the villages as doctors, doctors' assistants,
teachers, village-scribes, even as agricultural labourers, blacksmiths, wood-
cutters, and so on, and tried to live there in close contact with the peasants.
(IV, 357)

Takuboku's stanzas are controlled to convey the sense of frustration arising from the failure of the group to demonstrate their convictions through some positive social action. The refrain at the end
of each stanza, "But no one strikes the table with a clenched fist/
And shouts: 'For the people!' " emphasizes the vanity of the discussion. A stanza-by-stanza increase in intensity is achieved by moving
from an abstract, intellectual tone ("reading and debate") to convic-

tion ("We know"), to personal circumstances ("young"), and finally to concrete physical details ("candles," "the corpse of a small insect" in the cup, a particular young woman).

However, in spite of the dramatic presentation of the scene, the reader is left with the feeling that Takuboku has brought more rhetoric than conviction to the composition of the poem. If the poet-narrator is himself present at the discussion, and if he feels so strongly that some action should be taken, why does he not take the initiative and strike *his* fist on the table? One is not sure whether his criticism and frustration is directed at the group as a whole or if he is criticizing himself. Or was the poem perhaps intended for wider application? Does Takuboku fear that because of a lack of leadership all the high ideals of the movement will come to nothing, ending like the corpse of the small insect and leaving the adherents only fatigue as a reward for their zeal? In short, the poem gives the impression that it is merely a figment of Takuboku's fantasy stimulated by the book he had recently read. There is no record showing Takuboku's attending a meeting or gathering in which he participated in reading books on revolution and discussing them in the way described in the poem. The endless discussion he talks of is therefore a mere product of conceptualization. Takuboku has shown such an extraordinary ability to create an imaginary situation that the reader will be easily deceived into believing that the poet himself must have had an actual experience similar to the one portrayed in the poem. This ability is indeed one manifestation of Takuboku's genius, but a poem that has not grown out of the poet's actual emotional experience remains merely a poetic sketch of a situation created through the fabrication of fancy.[6]

Dealing in "A Spoonful of Cocoa" with a subject similar to that of "After Endless Discussions," Takuboku shows some slight improvement in his treatment of the subject. Going beyond the mere description of a situation, he draws the mind of a man:

> I know the terrorist's sorrowful heart—
> The heart in which words and act are united,
> The heart ready to speak through actions
> In place of the ineffectual words,
> The heart that flings body and soul at its enemies—
> And it is the sadness a serious and ardent man
>   always has.

> After endless discussions
> I sip a cold spoonful of cocoa.
> In the faint bitterness of its flavor
> I know a terrorist's sorrowful heart.

The first stanza has the same superficiality that we have seen in "After Endless Discussions." In the second stanza, however, through the image of a spoonful of cocoa and its flavor, Takuboku has made real the inexplicable loneliness the terrorist feels.

At the same time, however, one cannot eliminate entirely the feeling that the poem is artificial. Takuboku was neither a terrorist himself nor was there any terrorist in the circle of his friends. Again the situation presented in the poem is merely imaginary and theatrical. Therefore the loneliness that the poet says the terrorist feels does not go beyond the poet's rational assumption of the feeling. In the two poems discussed above Takuboku remains throughout an onlooker of the situation he has created, and because of its artificiality, devoid of the poet's genuine feelings, he has failed to convince the reader that his attempt at identifying himself with revolutionaries has come from his profound sympathy with them.

Takuboku's better handling of an image as a means of conveying particular feelings can be seen in "An Afternoon in My Study":

> I dislike the women of this land.
>
> On the rough paper
> Of a foreign book I am reading
> Wine was spilt by accident.
> Sad to see it not sinking in easily.
>
> I dislike the women of this land.

Takuboku's dissatisfaction with the women, who, for whatever reason, are slow in absorbing the new ideas necessary for the future of Japan, is compactly expressed in the second stanza. The vivid image of spilt wine too slow to soak into the page of the book enables the reader to have an immediate intellectual and emotional experience.

"An Airplane," which closes the series, is a good demonstration of Takuboku's artistic mastery. In this poem what Iwaki has pointed out—Takuboku using poems as social protest—is most apparent:

Look up! Today, again, in that blue sky
An airplane flies high.

On a Sunday, his rare day off,
A servant boy
Is at home with his consumptive mother
Alone, with tired eyes after hard study.

Look up! Today, again, in that blue sky
An airplane flies high.

In the use of simple language, Takuboku reveals his craftsmanship. With the minimum use of subjective expressions, for example ("Look up!" is the only subjective utterance), Takuboku has controlled the tone and images. Further, by using such a simple word as "again" in the first and last stanzas, Takuboku shows that the flight of the plane over the boy's head takes place every day; while the fact that his life is one of constant toil is related by the simple word "rare." The second stanza, which describes without comment the boy's daily life, is the poet's quiet voice of protest against the injustice of a society whose only recompense to a hard working, ambitious youth is a life of poverty.

The plane is used as a symbol of hope or the aspiration of the boy for a better life, something that may possibly be through his hard study won. By using the plane as a symbol of a better future, Takuboku thus shows a conviction that hard work and patient endurance will in the long run be rewarded; or at least Takuboku clings to the hope that such a possibility exists. The flight of the plane then functions as a means to keep the boy's vision directed upward lest it be lost in the hardship of life. The boy for whom the poet shows his compassion is of course his alter ego; Takuboku himself has been pursuing a new vision of the world. Read in this way, "An Airplane" is Takuboku's poetic expression of his own situation as well as his dream for the attainment of a better society in the future.

Many of Takuboku's verses indeed reveal one characteristic flaw apparent in all three periods of his poetic development: Takuboku's poetry, whether composed in the world of the Romantic idealist or of the revolutionary, too often reveals only a contrived conceptual outlook. Takuboku was, however, a conscientious poet constantly trying to make innovations in style and content in his attempt to perfect his craft. As we have seen above, there are a fair number of poems which document his steady improvement. With increased experience Takuboku gradually learned to develop a shorter, condensed poetic form in which the fusion of thought and feeling could be better accomplished. His constant endeavor to improve himself as a poet in the western style thus paved the way to his achievement in the tanka, a supremely compressed poetic form in which Takuboku demonstrates his full power as a poet.

CHAPTER 4

Self-portrait of a Young Artist

B ETWEEN 1906 and 1910 Takuboku tried his hand at prose fiction. Much of his work, however, consisting of no more than journal-like recountings of the author's personal experiences in Shibutami and Hokkaido, and lacking either well controlled plot or character development, is of little literary value. This does not mean, however, that Takuboku's stories should be altogether ignored, as many critics tend to do. True, his achievement as a novelist does not in any way approach that of Natsume Sōseki and Shimazaki Tōson, the accomplished contemporaries of Takuboku, but a few select works such as *The Hospital Window, The Shadow of a Bird* and *Our Gang and He* show Takuboku's potential in this genre, a potential hot yet fully developed when his brief life ended.

Takuboku began his novel writing in a burst of naive enthusiasm, not without a touch of arrogance. His zest for the novel is spelled out in his diary in an entry made during his brief stay in Tokyo in June, 1906:

I have read almost all the novels recently published. Among them only the works of Mr. Natsume Sōseki and Mr. Shimazaki Tōson, the two most erudite writers, are worth special attention. The others are worthless. Mr. Natsume has an extraordinary gift but lacks "greatness." Mr. Shimazaki is also a promising writer. *The Broken Commandment* certainly excels others but it is not the work of a genius. He is not a youth of vigorous revolutionary spirit. Anyhow, the novel is flourishing. . . . Sure enough, I was not wrong in my expectations. The decision, "I will write a novel," was the only souvenir I brought myself. (V, 102)

The consequence of this undisciplined exuberance left to us today includes novels and stories poorly planned and executed and many incomplete works. Takuboku was to come to a belated realization

99

that enthusiasm and self-confidence are not enough. In his prose fiction writing Takuboku jumped into the water before learning how to swim. The first chaotic results of his daring give an impression of frantic efforts just to keep afloat. As he became more at home in the new medium, however, he began to move about with grace and style. It is tempting to speculate what he might have achieved had he lived longer.

His attempts at writing novels without first carefully observing the characteristics peculiar to fiction led to the frustration of repeated rejection by publishers. He continued to write, however, confident that increased experience would lead to eventual mastery and the development of a style appropriate to his temperament. In time, his painstaking effort began to pay off, as can be seen in his gradual control of plot and development of character.

Takuboku's career as a novelist, short as it was, can be divided into three periods corresponding to the movements he was associated with. The first, his Romantic period, 1906–07, marks Takuboku's abrupt shift of interest from poetry to the novel. He believed that the novel more than poetry would enable him to give free vent to his Romantic imagination. Of the four pieces written in that year, three remain today: *Clouds Are Geniuses, The Funeral Procession* and *Drifting*.[1]

The second period, 1908–09, a year of apprenticeship in Naturalism, is represented by nine works: "Mr. Kikuchi," *The Hospital Window*, "Velvet," "Two Streams of Blood," *The Shadow of a Bird*, "Dysentery," "Footprints," "Sapporo" and "A Postcard." Through the influence of Naturalism, which stressed the importance of realistic observation of life, Takuboku began to improve his novel writing skills.

The third period, 1910, is characterized by Takuboku's rejection of Naturalism, clearly shown in his attempt at a new type of novel. From this period remain "The Road" and the posthumously published *Our Gang and He*, which marked the end of his career as a novelist. Between the time of the completion of this last work, probably written during May and June of 1910, and his death in April, 1912, Takuboku the writer devoted his creative energies mostly to his new field of interest, socialism.

Let us now examine the process of Takuboku's maturation as a novelist through a consideration of selected representative works from each of the three periods.

I *The First Period*

A. Clouds Are Geniuses

In an entry in his diary for July 3, 1906, Takuboku recorded his aspirations for this early work, an account remarkable for its vagueness of detail and overweening self-confidence: "In this novel I am going to write about the revolutionary spirit yet chaotically swirling in the heart of youth. Its theme and structure will probably be unprecedented: it is the bell of dawn announcing great revolutionary destruction. The hero is myself and strange characters keep appearing. While writing this, my spirit grew fantastically excited" (V, 102). Takuboku took the material of the novel from his experiences as a teacher at Shibutami Elementary School. Though he attempted to use the work as a vehicle for expressing his Romantic and revolutionary ideals, *Clouds Are Geniuses* is essentially an autobiographical novel. Takuboku must have completed the first draft in July; he revised it in November. The finished form is far from being "the bell of dawn announcing great revolutionary destruction," described in the diary. The young writer had yet to realize that it takes more than enthusiasm and confidence to produce a work of art.

The novel has two separate, loosely connected plots. The first part of the story dramatizes the protagonist's relationships with his fellow teachers, particularly the principal, of the school where he teaches; the second part centers on his dialogue with a stranger who shares his Romantic ideals.

Twenty-one-year-old Arata Kōsuke, the narrator as well as protagonist of the story, is teaching at a small country school. A youth of independent spirit and revolutionary ideas, he strives to broaden the perspective of his students beyond the conventional provincialism of the village. Since he is only a provisional uncertified teacher, he cannot teach the courses he really wants to teach: English and the history of Western civilization, and so he volunteers to teach them to upper class students as extracurricular courses without pay. The students, thirteen-to-sixteen year olds, are captivated by his fresh young enthusiasm. Aware of his influence on them, he uses these classes as an opportunity to indoctrinate the students with his own ideas about society, the evil of which Kōsuke believes is personified by the principal of the school, a helpless slave of convention and tradition. These two class hours have thus become for Kōsuke the high moments of his otherwise monotonous life at the school.

On this particular day, June 30, the principal has instructed Kōsuke to send the students home without the extra lessons because his wife, whom Kōsuke, for reasons of physical resemblance, calls Madame Potato, has a headache. Kōsuke has to obey; the principal's family, numbering four all together, live in a room adjacent to the teachers' room, and the extra classes would disturb the ailing woman. Kōsuke is instead ordered to fill the time compiling the monthly reports on grades, attendance, school lunches and other matters. Instead of the two hours of paradisal joy he had looked forward to, Kōsuke must endure an infernal agony of dull clerical rountine.

Kōsuke is further disgruntled when the principal, jealous of Kōsuke's popularity among the pupils, voices displeasure over a song Kōsuke has written which all the pupils are singing, a song so popular as to be regarded by many as the school song. The principal is angry not so much because the song has a revolutionary overtone but because of what he feels is a violation of protocol. He thinks that Kōsuke composed the song with the intention of making it the school song without first getting the approval of the principal, thereby ignoring the authority of the head of the school. Kōsuke's angry retort to the principal's accusation leads to a fierce argument between them. The quarrel ends abruptly when a woman teacher, who has sympathized with Kōsuke for some time, says simply: "Yesterday I borrowed the song from Sakae [a pupil] and copied it for myself. I don't understand music well, but I thought it was a fine song. In fact, I've decided to teach it to my children in the singing lesson tomorrow" (III, 14–15). The flag of victory is thus hoisted for Kōsuke, while the principal with a flushed face, trembling in anger, glares at him.

Before the storm of argument subsides completely, Kōsuke is handed a letter from a "beggar" who wishes to see him. Despite the strong objection of the principal, who in his vanity does not want a beggar loitering around his school, Kōsuke invites the man into the teachers' room. The "beggar" turns out to be a friend of Kōsuke's close friend, Amano Shuun, who lives in a neighboring town. The "beggar," Ishimoto Shunkichi, has called on Kōsuke with a letter of reference from Amano. Here the first half of the novel ends.

The second part of the story, occupying one third of the total number of pages in the novel, is dominated by Ishimoto's narrative. He has had a wretched life, not only because of poverty but also because he has only one eye. His life took a turn for the better, however, when he met Amano. Amano, until recently a teacher like Kōsuke, has lost his position after quarreling with his principal and is now living in extreme poverty in a house "filthier than a pig sty." Yet to Ishimoto (and to Kōsuke as well) Amano's life is blessed with true wealth, a richness of idealism and of confidence in human ability to endure and overcome the difficulties of life so as to create a better world to live in. Amano's brotherly affection and understanding have given Ishimoto the courage to confront poverty without fear. Thus strengthened, Ishimoto has decided to become a beggar in order to return to his old home in the country to care for his sick mother. Amano and Ishimoto had separated in tears, and the story Ishimoto tells brings tears to the eyes not only of Kōsuke but also the woman teacher who has been attentively listening to it close by.

Although *Clouds Are Geniuses* shows the enthusiasm that went into its production, its many flaws are obvious. The language is affected, and exaggerated expressions are embarassing to the reader. It is ludicrous indeed to see that the protagonist in all seriousness regards himself as a leader of a great revolution like the French Revolution and sees his pupils as being Jacobins. Furthermore, as the author jumps the track of the plot, the reader is left with two serious unanswered questions: Is Takuboku attempting to satirize or caricature the establishment as represented by the principal, apparently the major point of the first part, or is he attempting to set forth a Romantic, if not revolutionary, idealism that will be realized by individuals of "genius"? Takuboku's own comment on the novel described above seems to indicate that his original intention was to answer the second question; yet the novel in its final form is an infelicitous combination of two different treatments of his material. His failure to work out a method of blending the two ideas has resulted in a novel containing two unrelated plots.

In addition, the characterization of Kōsuke, Ishimoto and Amano is flat; they are types rather than people, mere mouthpieces for the author to express his Romantic views of poverty and genius, tradition and the educational system. These exaggerated stereotypes remain stagnant from the beginning to the end of the novel. In short, Takuboku failed to create a character who, while representing the author's own perspective on social issues, has his own distinct place in the novel. Amano is too much like Kōsuke, who in turn too obviously resembles Takuboku himself.

Despite all these conspicuous flaws, *Clouds Are Geniuses* does contain some points of strength. Takuboku built a successful contrast between two opposing groups. The principal and his wife are confined forever to the narrow scope of village life. The three idealistic young men, Kōsuke, Amano and Ishimoto, all facing poverty and loss of social position, personify the free spirit, conscience and compassion of humanity concerned with the welfare of the world. Their philosophy of life is summed up by Amano:

Unless one drinks up even the dregs of the misfortunes of life, one cannot become a true man. Life is a long dark tunnel; here and there there are only the forests of skeletons called cities. One should avoid straying into them lest one forget the exit of the tunnel. Under the feet there runs the stream of eternal sorrow and pain; it has been flowing probably since before the birth of human life. Do not step back even if your direction is hindered by the stream; if you do, the dark hole grows all the darker. Death or marching on—you have to choose one of the two. Advancement is battle. . . . In the existing society what can escape from the blow of the hatchet of destruction? Today's world cannot be improved without its total destruction. Leaving the great work of reconstruction to the genius who is to come after us, we, for the time being, must swing the hatchet of devastation all the way down to the heart of the matter. (III, 32)

Amano's statement articulates the author's own revolutionary vision, though what comprises the society which needs to be destroyed is not clearly defined. The genius is the one sensitive enough to comprehend social evils and the necessity of their destruction, and is willing to take action in order to realize his ideal. Clearly Takuboku tries to present Arata Kōsuke, namely himself, as the genius Amano speaks of. Examined in this light, the allegorical significance of the protagonist's name becomes obvious: *"Ara"* (new) *"ta"* (field) *"Kō"* (cultivate) *"suke"* (man). The group to which the protagonist belongs, then, represents the new era which will supersede the one represented by the principal and his wife.

Stylistically, *Clouds Are Geniuses* demonstrates Takuboku's precocious mastery of descriptive writing, which eventually comes to full bloom in his tanka. Caricatures of the principal and his wife reveal his sharp humorous imagination:

The mustache below his nose has no lustre; this is evidence of complete lack of vitality in the person. Both ends of the mustache have come down, like those of an eel, all the way down to his jaw. This is probably a symbol of the spirit that has forgotten aspiration. . . . He has three moles all together, the largest of which is below the left eye placed like an ominous star. How unsightly it is! This is what is commonly called a "tear mole," and fortunately my family and kin or the people I respect do not ordinarily have it on their faces. . . . In short, I have drawn a conclusion: Principal Tashima=0. (III, 5–6)

Takuboku thus uses the physical appearance of the principal as a metaphor for his character. This passage, though damaged by affected language, is one of the more successful ones in which Takuboku has created a vivid image of a character who otherwise tends to remain a mere type.

The principal's wife is caricatured with more biting cynicism, and the description of her becomes more lively than that of her husband:

The paper screen door behind us was opened abruptly and, draped in a finely-striped cotton kimono reeking of sweat and fastened only with a small string, her breasts exposed to suckle the child in her arms, quietly appeared a ghost. It is the entrance of Madame Potato. . . . Staring sharply at me with her upturned needle-like eyes, she stood by her husband. If one could express the sound of the grinding teeth of a dying woman in hell by something visible in this world, the woman who, with her dry gray hair thinned like thorns, is holding the bones of her child in both hands, the expression of Madame Potato's eyes when she stared at me would be it.

The living goddess—of privation?—stood silent like a stone stature. (III, 12)

The stylistic strength of the novel is, however, undercut by Takuboku's abuse of exaggeration. Caricature too easily slips into affected hyperbole. When Takuboku in the second half of the novel, uses an exaggerated style which is supposed to be more serious, it almost results in a caricature of the protagonist. In his letter to Kōsuke, Amano refers to the fact that Ishimoto has lost one eye. On reading this, Kōsuke begins to imagine Ishimoto as a Napoleon who lost one eye bravely fighting at the battle of Waterloo. Though the young man standing in front of him in no way approximates the fantasy of the military leader, actualities do nothing to curb Kōsuke's soaring imagination. On the contrary, Ishimoto in his shabby outfit becomes for Kōsuke a reincarnation of John the Baptist: "One day, one time, he must have got his silvery voice with irregular sound from the prophet in the wilderness, who lived on locusts and wild honey with the skin of a camel on his body" (III, 24).

The title of the novel fits well with its content and theme. The clouds can be interpreted as drifters, appearing one moment and disappearing the next. The "clouds" in the novel are Amano, Ishimoto and particularly Kōsuke, who, it is implied, finding no peace of mind nor happiness in the tradition bound village life, will eventually, with his potential for genius, become a wanderer like the other two. The title of the story is highly Romantic, and appropriately so, for what the story itself deals with is a Romanticized world of both humor and pathos. Yet the irony—to be sure, an irony unintended by Takuboku—is that while a trace of the author's genius is apparent in the work, the novel itself leaves the reader in the clouds: to paraphrase a common Japanese saying, it leaves the same confusion as results from the attempt to grab a cloud.

B.   The Funeral Procession

By the time he came to write *The Funeral Procession*, his third novel, Takuboku had learned that a certain distance must be maintained between the author himself and the characters he creates. As a result *The Funeral Procession*, a better controlled novel than *Clouds Are Geniuses*, demonstrates Takuboku's increased mastery of composition.

The plot of *The Funeral Procession* is rather simple. Tachibana Kōichi, the narrator-protagonist of the story, is a history teacher after five years' absence just returned to the city of Morioka, "the sleeping city," where he had spent his childhood. He is surprised at the many changes that have taken place in the city: new bookstores similar to those in Tokyo adorn the main street; the capitol has been rebuilt of concrete in western fashion; an electric power company has gone up; school girls are wearing shoes instead of traditional *geta*; and a restaurant with western facade offers a western menu. Morioka is a microcosm of rapidly changing Meiji Japan. No matter how different its appearance, however, to Kōichi it is still "the beautiful city of memory." His conviction is confirmed by the sight of an autumn sunset, which presents the intrinsic natural beauty of the city in all its glory.

One day on the way to his old school he sees a beggar woman holding a child, sitting by the bridge near the gate of the school. Without giving her any special notice, he goes into the building in hopes of seeing a former teacher. Disappointed, he walks back to the gate where he suddenly hears children shouting, "A funeral! A funeral!". Six men are coming slowly down the road, two of them carrying a coffin wrapped in white cloth and tied with straw ropes. As they approach the bridge, the beggar woman jumps up and rushes screaming to the procession, one arm around her child and the other raised trying to reach the coffin. The man in the front of the procession kicks her to the ground.

Kōichi learns that the funeral is that of the madman Shigeru and the grieving beggar is the madwoman Onatsu. These names bring back the memory of a scene he had witnessed five years earlier.

While taking a stroll through a field early one autumn morning he had come to the fence of a shrine. At the fence he had watched unseen while Shigeru and Onatsu danced hand in hand in the yard in front of the shrine. With smiles of exultation on their faces they danced under a gigantic ginko tree. The tree, as if to bless the dancing couple below, began to shed its leaves, themselves dancing in the air upon them. The red-gold of the rising sun, the golden yellow of the falling leaves and the joyful flushed faces of the dancing couple were blended into a perfect unity. Kōichi, sole witness to the event, had stood motionless, drunk with the beauty and solemnity of the occasion. This is the scene which at the funeral procession comes back to him.

The part of the story which describes the "mad" dance of Shigeru and Onatsu redeems an otherwise tediously developed novel. The first part of the story is more like a journal documenting a young man's impressions of various changes that have taken place in the city. A careful reading of the whole work, however, reveals Takuboku's efforts to sustain a single unified idea. The dance scene illuminates the reason for the apparently pointless accounts of the changing city in the first part of the novel.

Labeled as "mad" by a society devoid of sympathy and under-standing, Shigeru and Onatsu are social outcasts. Yet Kōichi's Romantic imagination elevates them to the level of divinity precisely because of this madness. The narrator, watching the ecstatic dance of the two "mad" people, transforms them in his imagination into sanctified dancers in the garden of the gods:

The reviving voice like the gods' smile flowed in heaven: the morning breeze began to blow. Then, as the giant ginko tree started tearing off the golden cloud, its clothes, as in the olden time when Zeus appeared in disguise, the rain of gold fell upon the two. Ah . . . ! thousands and thousands of small golden dancing fans, tangled and untangled, kept falling upon them, burying their bodies. Some of them, as if manipulated by unseen threads, not returning to the branches whence they came, were giving themselves to the shining wind. The dance of leaves in the sky and the dance of man on earth! Madman Shigeru and madwoman Onatsu were dancing the earthly dance in the garden of the gods. (III, 54–55)

The innocence and purity that links Shigeru and Onatsu makes their relationship a truly human one in terms of honesty, acceptance and complete trust. They are indeed heaven's elect; and their madness is the madness of possession by the gods, a true manifestation of their genuine humanity. Quoting Plato the narrator further remarks: "A madman is heaven's prodigy" (III, 55).

The message of the scene is clearly shown in Kōichi's changed attitude toward the beggar woman who rushes to the coffin of her beloved. His sympathy is with Onatsu, who, torn by deep sorrow, desperately tries to cling to the goodness of life she had experienced with Shigeru. In Kōichi's eyes she is no longer merely a mad beggar, an object of ridicule, but a woman of warmth, compassion and love whose mourning is the cry of humanity.

Here the connection between the two parts of the story becomes clear. In the first part, while describing the many changes in the city, the narrator often emphasizes that some things have not changed at all. The beauty of the city is for him epitomized by the rain of an autumn evening: this beauty makes Morioka what it is. The inherent beauty of this city parallels the beauty of Shigeru and Onatsu. Though they experienced changes in themselves which led to madness, the fundamental beauty of their humanity itself never changed. Shining through their madness, this joyous humanity burst into full light at the shrine, and their dance was the celebration of it.

Another factor linking the two parts of the story is Takuboku's use of memory, or rather his efforts to find meaning in reminiscence of the past. He devotes many pages to having the narrator describe his childhood memories: his frequent visits to the Kozukata Castle in the city; the day when he was told by an older friend that he resembled Napoleon; and the time he thought about becoming like Byron, who gave up his pen for a sword. The city of Morioka is for the narrator thus "the beautiful city of memory" in which he can find his identity. The scene of the ecstatic dance is also a memory, one that has awakened the narrator's awareness of certain values in life. Like the memories of his childhood, the memory of the extraordinary experience gives him as a grown man a sense of pleasure and fulfillment. In both cases memory preserves unchanging values the narrator can cherish, giving a sense of order and permanence to life and leading him to a fuller self-knowledge. Takuboku also expresses this idea elsewhere: "The days gone by are always longed for by all. The past is the best means in the world by which to know ourselves. The passions of longing for the past eventually enable us, through the shadow cast behind, to grasp our own present image, which is also linked with tomorrow" (IV, 74).

Although the style of *The Funeral Procession* is still affected and amateurish, one recognizes an improvement in plot development and characterization. Takuboku has begun to grasp the significance of keeping personal elements under control, making of *The Funeral Procession* a more polished work.

II *The Second Period*

A. The Hospital Window

Modeled after the Naturalistic novel, *The Hospital Window* indeed has the gloomy tone characteristic of that genre. The modern critic Kubokawa Tsurujirō maintains that this novel was the first to establish Takuboku's place as a Naturalistic novelist.[2] Yet a careful analysis of the work indicates that the author was attempting more than just an imitation. In fact, Takuboku's principal interest in this novel appears to lie less in creating a work in the vein of the conventional Naturalistic novel than in experimenting with a novel of a new kind, if not a psychological novel itself then a type of novel anticipatory of that genre. In the history of the modern Japanese novel, Takuboku is certainly one of the earliest to attempt the psychological novel.

The plot of the novel centers around the protagonist Nomura Ryōkichi, who had formerly attempted to establish himself as a poet and is currently situated as a reporter for a local newspaper at Kushiro in Hokkaido. To the office at which he works, a new man, Takeyama, a former acquaintance of Nomura, has just come as editor. Nomura is not happy to see him, not only because he now has to work under a man six years his junior but also because Takeyama knows Nomura's past. Four years earlier both had been in Tokyo striving for recognition as poets. They had come from the same prefecture and were by chance living in the same lodging house. They became acquainted when Takeyama's first collection of poetry was published, thereby establishing his reputation as a promising poet overnight. Takeyama can recall that Nomura, introspective and withdrawn, had made some claim to being a hypnotist. Nomura had also then professed to be a Christian and wished to write a poem or novel dealing with the conflict of body and soul, reality and ideal. At the same time there had been rumors that Nomura was only pretending to be a Christian as a means of seducing young girls and even married women. Recollections of Nomura's past then are unpleasant. Nomura must face the memories as well as the present reality of the weakness of his character, of which he himself is more acutely aware than anyone else.

Though his anxiety is unwarranted, Nomura feels that his position is threatened by Takeyama's arrival. Nomura is especially disturbed when Takeyama soon after taking over his new post employs another person for Nomura's department, one from their mutual home prefecture, in fact. This leads Nomura to believe that Takeyama intends to dismiss him. Nomura does not realize that his apprehension comes from his own basic nature: he is a withdrawn, unsociable person, timid and fearful. His fear of losing his post increases daily; he is convinced that conversations between the editor and other members of the staff are concerned with the immediate elimination of his position and that it is only a matter of days before he will be told to resign. In short, he has become paranoic. He grows more withdrawn than ever, with the air of a wounded animal cornered by hunters.

Nomura, now twenty-nine years old, has been living a lonely bachelor life sharing a six-mat [9' x 12'] room with a young man working at the post office, who has a peculiar habit of sleeping with his eyes half open as if to observe Nomura's behavior. Nomura spends his monthly salary on sake and cigarettes as soon as he receives it. He obtains the necessities of life by running up debts, which he has no intention of paying, at various shops and restaurants. His rent is two months in arrears, and in order to escape from the landlady's nagging about it he loiters in the city every evening, returning to his lodging only after everyone else in the house is asleep. One evening, in order to get money for supper, he blackmails the wife of the owner of a clothing store where one of the employees has recently died. Nomura had heard a rumor that the wife had abused the clerk and driven her to death. Nomura takes advantage of the situation and satisfies his hunger with illicit gains.

There are two pastimes Nomura genuinely enjoys. One is to visit a hospital near his office. Whenever he wants to smoke or drink sake or just listen to the cheerful voices of young women, he goes to the hospital where he knows he can get free cigarettes and sake from the doctors and nurses. His frequent visits have a further significance for Nomura as they provide him with the opportunity to be master of a situation: he can gain control over others through hypnotism, which he practices on the nurses. The second source of pleasure is his verse writing. His ambition is to create a poem in the vein of Milton's *Paradise Lost*; but though he has been pouring his energy and imagination into it for a long time, he has so far written only a few lines. On the evening when he blackmails the dress shop owner's wife, returning home late he attempts to continue work on his poem about the Fall of man. Sensing his roommate's half-open eyes on his back, he is trapped into an examination of his own heart and becomes frightened by the lines he himself has written:

> Son of man has no time to sleep.
> Ah, the hue of the angry cloud
> Announces the Day of Judgment. (III, 98)

The poem he writes is the cry of his own fear. Uncritical of the quality of the verse, he is aware only that it leads him to self-scrutiny and despair: he sees himself as a sinner like Cain, conscious always of the eyes of an angry God. Thus the verse writing which was once a source of delight for him has turned into a ruthless reminder of his own sinfulness. Frightened by his own vision of judgment, Nomura rushes out of the lodging house toward the hospital. Coming near, he spots the lighted window of a room where a nurse is getting ready for bed. Nomura stops and stares at the young woman through the window unaware that he himself is being watched by Takeyama, who boards at a house across from the hospital.

Without the slightest idea that his improper conduct has been

witnessed by Takeyama, Nomura confronts the editor on the following morning to learn Takeyama's intentions for his future. No
clear answer coming from the editor, Nomura feels all the more
uncertain of his position. Out of desperation he protests to
Takeyama that he is working hard day and night. Nomura tells
Takeyama that he walked around the city until late the night before
trying to gather news. Takeyama, who knows that Nomura is lying,
replies with a sneer: "How was the window of the hospital?". These
words are the final blow: Nomura's anguished cry—"Oh, God! Oh,
God!"—closes the novel.

The most glaring flaw of *The Hospital Window* is of course the
characterization of Takeyama, too close to the author himself. References to the character's physical resemblance to Napoleon and to
his credentials both as an editor and poet obviously originate from
the author's narcissistic bent to dramatize himself.

In Nomura, however, Takuboku has created a believable character who represents a soul in conflict "fatigued by the endless struggle with life." Withdrawn and reticent, with a poetic, fragile sensibility, Nomura represents a decadent hero, a character anticipatory
of Ōba Yōzō in Dazai Osamu's *No Longer Human*, published over
forty years later. Nomura drifts from day to day, his moral integrity
corroded by desperation and fatigue. His constant feeling of anxiety
increases his vulnerability to the desires of the flesh, thereby compounding his sense of hopelessness. There exists no possibility of
redeeming himself: Nomura recognizes that he is in this dilemma
because of a lack of real faith in God. He has only a fear of God, a
vision of an angry judge. His knowledge of the Christian faith thus
ironically alienates him from God and from the world he lives in,
and gives rise to constant self-accusation, which in turn encourages
further immorality. He is trapped in a vicious cycle of remorse and
the repetition of despicable acts, which are precipitated by the remorse itself.

Takuboku, himself not a Christian, explores no further than
Nomura's despair, with the result that the novel is dominated by
gloom. The tone of hopelessness by which Nomura is haunted is
well sustained by a dramatic use of eye imagery. The eyes of Nomura's roommate, half open even in sleep, symbolize the stare of the
world, indifferent to the suffering of an individual yet casting a cold
eye on his human failings. It is Takeyama's eyes that see Nomura's
secretive spying at the window of the hospital. Takeyama uses this

incident as a means to reprimand Nomura just when he is most in need of support. Thus Takeyama's eyes also come to represent the stare of a merciless world. To Nomura all these eyes, accompanied by his deep sense of guilt, become the ever-watchful eyes of an indignant God focused on his whole life.

Considering the fact that Takuboku wrote this novel after less than two years' apprenticeship, *The Hospital Window* is a remarkable accomplishment. Kubokawa considers it "one of the best works Takuboku has written, a work that guarantees Takuboku's place as a novelist."[3] With the publication of this work Takuboku became more confident of his ability to establish himself as a novelist, a confidence that was vindicated when a later novel was accepted by a major newspaper.

B.   The Shadow of a Bird

The Shadow of a Bird was serialized sixty days in the Tokyo *Mainichi* newspaper in November and December of 1908. This was Takuboku's first and last attempt at writing a novel for a newspaper. As we can see from his diary, the novel was a reworking of an earlier manuscript entitled *Shizuko's Sorrow:*

> I pulled out the old manuscript of *Shizuko's Sorrow*, but I could tell it was no good. Exaggerated and rudimentary. So I decided to change the whole design, make it more complex and profound, and rewrote it. But I couldn't come up with a proper title. Last night I tried *The Corpse of a Bird* but that didn't seem right. After agonizing over it I finally decided on *The Shadow of a Bird.* (V, 343–44)

Since the original manuscript of *Shizuko's Sorrow* is lost, it is impossible to tell what the initial story was, how it was developed, or how much Takuboku revised it. Nevertheless, the passage quoted above clearly shows a different novelist from the Takuboku of the previous year. He is becoming a more competent critic of his own work, with a keen eye for its weaknesses.

The novel centers on a group of young people in a small village during the summer vacation homecoming of Ogawa Shingo, the oldest son of a wealthy family of the village, currently a student majoring in English at a university in Tokyo. The story begins with a scene in which Shingo's sister, Shizuko, the oldest daughter of the family comes with their two younger sisters and a servant to the railroad station to welcome her brother. Shizuko is the young widow of an army lieutenant killed during the Russo-Japanese war. Now, against her wishes, her parents are attempting to arrange a marriage between Shizuko and her dead husband's brother. Shizuko believes that only her brother, Shingo, can empathize with her and persuade her parents to give up this marriage arrangement. At first Shingo says he will not come home for the summer; so when he finally decides to return after all, Shizuko is convinced that her pleading letter prompted his change of mind.

When Shingo at first hesitates to return home for the summer, Shizuko immediately thinks that her brother wants to avoid meeting Kiyoko, her close friend and his former girl friend, now married to Katō, a local physician. Shizuko believes that Kiyoko was the one who broke off the relationship and that Shingo still loves her. As soon as Shingo appears in the novel, however, the reader is informed that it is rather Shingo's cold rejection of Kiyoko that brought about the breach. Shingo does not feel comfortable at the prospect of meeting Kiyoko again, but he is displeased with himself to see that he feels awkward toward her. He tells himself that he is the stronger, that he is the winner, for having refused to take Kiyoko as his wife. When the marriage arrangement was pending between Kiyoko and Katō, Kiyoko had expressed her willingness to refuse the proposal for the sake of Shingo, but at the last moment he turned away from her. Remembering the incident Shingo feels proud of himself. He returns to the village determined to try to make Kiyoko long for him always even though he himself does not have any affection for her. He has decided to become friendly with Katō in order to meet Kiyoko as frequently as possible. In his morbid arrogance Shingo wishes even to make Kiyoko weep in front of him. His sadistic pleasure would be similar to that of a cat manipulating a mouse before devouring it. Shingo has changed during his year in Tokyo and Shizuko senses that his brotherly congeniality has cooled.

Shingo comes to know Hinata Chieko, a school teacher, at a card party held in honor of his return, and on the following day calls on her at her lodging house. He brings her a few translated works of Ibsen along with a periodical in which his own short critical essay on Ibsen is printed; in exchange he borrows from her a translation of Renan's *Life of Christ*. He continues to visit her frequently, and acts as if he has great respect for her, always leading the topic of their conversation to such sophisticated subjects as the problems of life, faith and literary creation. Yet Chieko on her part cannot rid herself of the first unfavorable impression she formed of Shingo when she met him at the school two days after his return to the village. Chieko's misgivings concerning Shingo are justified; the shallowness of his regard for her is shown by the fact that he frequently visits her fellow teacher, Kamiyama Tomie, on the same day that he visits Chieko.

Twenty-one-year-old Chieko was employed to teach at this village school following her graduation from the Normal School in Morioka, the prefectural capital. She had entered the Ochanomizu Women's School in Tokyo at the age of fifteen, but upon the sudden death of her father the following year had been forced to return to her brother's home in Morioka. Her brother was indifferent to Chieko's interests and did nothing to help her return to the school in Tokyo. She then began to go to a Christian church, and, shortly after her mother's death and against her brother's wishes, was baptized. She made up her mind to be independent and entered the Normal School. Now she is lodging at the widow Oriyo's almost as a member of the family. Knowing the poverty of the family (Oriyo's first husband simply disappeared and the second was executed for his violation of military regulations during the Russo-Japanese war), Chieko ungrudgingly gives them financial aid from her meager monthly income.

Her fellow teacher Tomie is twenty-eight years old and married; but for the past three years she has been living alone, returning to be with her husband, himself a school teacher in Morioka, only for the New Year holidays. Although her background is mysterious, the villagers find her simple, sociable and congenial because of her gregarious nature. She is the favorite of Shingo's mother, Oryū, a former geisha.

The relationships among the various young characters become more involved when another character enters the scene. One day Shizuko sees the shadow of a bird crossing a paper screen door. An old saying has it that on the day when one sees the shadow of a bird an important visitor will come. Yoshino Mantarō, an artist friend of Shingo's, comes from Tokyo as his house guest.

After a few days' stay at the village, Mantarō decides to call on a friend from his art school days who is now teaching at a middle school in Morioka. At the station by chance he meets Chieko, who is going to Morioka also to visit a friend. The man Mantarō is to visit turns out to be the brother of Chieko's friend, and Mantarō and Chieko stay overnight at their place and return to the village together the next day. Shingo's displeasure soars high when he discovers that Mantarō and Chieko have become acquainted without his introduction.

On the following day, Shizuko's aunt from Morioka, who is helping to arrange her marriage, visits the Ogawas. In the evening the mayor of the village and other friends of the family join the Ogawas for a party. Mantarō, their house guest, is of course included, too. Sake flows freely, and in the course of the party Mantarō steps out of the house for a breath of fresh air. Strolling to the Tsurukai Bridge, he sees Chieko, who has come there with some children to catch fireflies. The children follow Mantarō and Chieko down into a shallow part of the river; but Oriyo's five-year-old boy slips, and the quick flow of the water carries him downstream. Mantarō dashes to save the boy, and in the excitement caused by the accident the mutual affection between Mantarō and Chieko surfaces.

Now there is a wall between Shingo and Mantarō. Jealous of Mantarō, Shingo entertains the idea of proposing marriage to Chieko, but his pride does not let him. He tells himself that she is only a country school teacher, beneath him in social position; but at the same time he does not want any other man to have the beautiful and intelligent young woman. Shingo is further disgruntled to observe that his sister Shizuko is also attracted to Mantarō. He ponders over a way to force Mantarō to return to Tokyo soon.

Then comes the day of the Obon festival, the day when the villagers enjoy themselves with the traditional dances. In the early evening Shingo visits Chieko. He opens the conversation on an ostensibly intellectual note, criticizing scholars of the day and attacking various schools of painters (no doubt with Mantarō in mind), but his arrogance is beginning to surface when suddenly he declares his affection for Chieko. She remains unmoved. Shingo, in an attempt to find out if Chieko loves Mantarō, says to her: "I sincerely wish for you and Yoshino the greatest happiness. Will you accept my congratulations?". He is clinging to the hope that Chieko will deny any relation with Mantarō, thereby leaving open the possibility of gaining her. But Chieko, blushing, calmly replies: "Thank you very much" (III, 288). His pride crushed, Shingo leaves Chieko at once and goes to visit Tomie.

In the meantime, tired of waiting for Shingo to return, Shizuko goes to watch the dancing with Mantarō, her sisters and the servants. Though she enjoys walking with Mantarō she cannot forget that at home the go-between for her marriage is conferring with her aunt. Picking up Chieko and Kiyoko, and wondering where Shingo is, they all go together to see the dance. Chieko, however, is not well, and though reluctant to leave Mantarō with Shizuko, is compelled by her illness to return home. Before leaving she informs Mantarō of Shingo's visit to her, and asks him to visit her the next day.

An hour or so after Shizuko and Mantarō come home, Shingo returns also, having slipped out the back door of Tomie's. Fatigued and irritated, he comes in just as Shizuko is coming out of Mantarō's room, where she had gone to express her concern over Shingo's absence. Enraged, Shingo begins to slap her. Alarmed by the noise, everyone, including Mantarō, rushes into the room to restrain Shingo. Humiliated and angry at Chieko's frank refusal of him, Shingo has used first Tomie and now Shizuko to vent his frustration.

The novel ends hastily with all the characters returning to their own places, all in different directions. Mantarō and Chieko go to Morioka, where Chieko, after recovering from dysentery, is hospitalized for tuberculosis. Mantarō is determined to stay there and help her, even though it means a professional sacrifice for him. Shingo leaves for Tokyo; and Shizuko, visiting her old friend Kiyoko, finds that she has misjudged her. Together Shizuko and Kiyoko lament over the vulnerability of women.

Kubokawa holds that *The Shadow of a Bird* is one of Takuboku's best novels.[4] Though the obvious flaws in the work lead the reader to question Kubokawa's appraisal, it must be admitted that the novel contains a number of strong points. The characterizations of Shingo. Shizuko and especially Chieko clearly demonstrate Takuboku's mastery in creating believable characters rather than types. Furthermore, the plot is carefully developed through the complicated relations of these characters.

However, the most disconcerting problem is that Takuboku failed to bring out clearly what he wished to say in the novel. His failure to focus on one point has contributed to the poor character development of Mantarō, whom Takuboku undoubtedly intended to present as one of the major characters, if not the protagonist, of the novel. We see the abnegation of Mantarō as a contrast to Shingo's egoism; but the theme most strongly associated with him is that of the loneliness and alienation of city life, as brought out in his conversation with Chieko at the Tsurukai Bridge:

On the fierce battlefield of city life, in which I have no leisure even to dream, I am pushed into loneliness by the endless pressure and stimulation. It is then that I am seized with the strong consciousness of my existence. The consciousness is certainly painful. Painful, but a different life is lived on that turbulent battlefield, isn't it? . . . Yet coming out to the country is a different story. In the country the romantic quiet is still preserved; dreams are here. Lyrics are in the country. A few minutes ago I was walking by myself and felt strongly that even though I was alone in this serene vast universe, the feeling was strangely more or less one of joy. . . . And the air in this environment is so romantic that everything appears like a dream. . . . Whenever I become smothered, I run out into the country, as I did this time. (III, 264)

The passage, which reeks of Romantic sentimentalism for country life, stands out unrelated to the rest of the novel. Kubokawa maintains that the passage sums up the theme of the novel,[5] but there is no development of the idea, particularly in relation to Mantarō, either before or after the passage. As a result the reader is not prepared to take it seriously. Takuboku perhaps wanted to make a point about the impersonality and loneliness of city life and pastoral quality of village life, but the reader knows that Mantarō's view of country life is illusory: the ugliness of city life characterized by "fierce battlefield" exists in the country also, different only in kind. Is Mantarō too much blinded by his Romantic fascination with rusticity to realize that fact? The whole point of the passage is confusing.

Takuboku must have felt the pressure of his time limit: he was given only sixty days of serialization by the *Mainichi* newspaper, which probably accounts for the abrupt ending of the novel. One should think that with enough time provided, Takuboku would have smoothed out the problems cited above. It is unfortunate that he was not given that opportunity.

III   *The Third Period*

A.   Our Gang and He

Our Gang and He, written probably in May and early June of 1910, was published posthumously with the help of Toki Aika in the

Yomiuri newspaper from August to September, 1912. As Odagiri Hideo says, the novel, though incomplete, is the best piece of prose fiction to come from Takuboku.[6] The novel develops a theme hinted at in the character of Mantarō in *The Shadow of a Bird:* the dilemma of the individual given to excessive introspection.

The story is narrated by a young newspaper reporter, one of an elite group of the better educated members of the staff. The story develops around the relationship between this group, "our gang," and a mysterious man, Takahashi Hikotarō, who always maintains a certain distance from others. The curiosity of the members of the gang is aroused by this quiet, withdrawn individual, and they delight in speculating about him. One of them imagines that Takahashi is perhaps a rebel against the establishment because his physical features resemble those of a physical education teacher of the reporter's middle school days who instigated a strike against the principal. Another, convinced by Takahashi's reticence, suspects that he is a henpecked husband.

Finally a day comes when they can get to know the real man. During a long and tedious meeting of the department where "our gang" and Takahashi work, they engage in conversation with him for the first time. Further, the narrator invites Takahashi out for a drink, and when it is too late for Takahashi to catch the last train, invites him to spend the night at his house. The hours the narrator and Takahashi spend together serve as an icebreaker, and gradually a friendship begins to develop between them. From this point on the story centers on the narrator's relation with Takahashi, particularly on their exchange of ideas about the trends of modern Japanese society and about the individual's place in that society.

The more the narrator listens to Takahashi talk about his life experience the more he realizes that the latter is a serious man of sensibility who has been struggling silently to find his place in a society characterized by sudden and rapid change. Takahashi, unable to find his place in the society, is acutely aware of his alienation, an alienation he senses as arising from his perceptiveness of the dilemma modern society faces. Takahashi's insight into "the disease of the age" leaves an especially strong impression on the narrator. Takahashi maintains that the modern world exists with a huge crack in the middle, the split brought about because of the fact that the new world and the old have not yet discovered a way to blend harmoniously. The "crack" of the age is, Takahashi believes, most apparent in the spiritual life of the Japanese people where it was caused by the rise of the consciousness of self, thereby producing a new sensibility with an inherent paradox: that one is made aware of the uncertainty of life, of alienation and loneliness through awareness of one's own individuality. The saddest aspect of the situation is that people must live with the crack without knowing how to mend it. The dilemma of modern man, then, is twofold: it involves the alienation of the newer and older elements *within* society and also the alienation of the individual *from* this disjointed society. In such a dilemma the idea of universal happiness is a delusion. Takahashi lives therefore only as a "sacrifice" for the next generation, living simply so as to die simply. For this kind of existence what a man needs is "a cold iron heart" which will function as a protecting shield against the disjointed world.

Not long after the evening spent with the narrator, Takahashi begins to devote his time and energy to helping Matsunaga, an illustrator of their newspaper. Matsunaga had become the pupil of a master of traditional Japanese painting while attending an art school. When he began to devote himself to oil painting, however, he was cast off by the master. After this expulsion he found employment as an illustrator, completely giving up his ambition to become an oil painter. Now he has contracted tuberculosis and it has developed to such an advanced stage that he cannot continue to work. Takahashi's silent inner struggle has nurtured his capacity to empathize with a fellow human being defeated by a topsy-turvy world. As if forgetting his own work, Takahashi does all he can to assist not only Matsunaga but also Matsunaga's old mother, who lives with him. Matsunaga, however, finally decides to return with his mother to their home village in the hope of recovering from his illness there. Takahashi and "our gang" send them off at the station, knowing well that they are seeing Matsunaga for the last time.

After Matsunaga's departure, all are back to routine except Takahashi. One member of "our gang" discovers by accident that Takahashi has been frequenting a movie theater in Asakusa, the amusement quarter of Tokyo. Just as the narrator has finished hearing this story from his colleague, Takahashi himself pays a call on the narrator and explains to both of the men the "mystery" of his recent maneuvering. He goes to the movies not for entertainment but to be free from the criticism of others and his own self-examination:

If I had money and free time, I would go somewhere, away from people as much as possible. Nature does not criticize us; yet at the same time it is too indifferent to us. It pays no attention to us even if we go into it. So a person like me, if he goes to the mountains or the sea, grows easily bored and has nothing to do but to begin to analyze himself. Compared with that, watching a motion picture is far better. Up until now I thought that time goes fast for a newspaper reporter, but the motion picture is faster. It skips the unnecessary parts. . . . On top of that, in a movie the speed of walking is nearly as fast as our running. Running is for sure incomparably fast. When I watch such a motion picture, my mind is always on the alert. While in a theater, not only am I in a place where nobody criticizes me but also I have no time for self-examination. These days, I wish I could spend my whole life with such a feeling as I get in watching a motion picture. (III, 406)

Judging from what he has accomplished, one can see that Takuboku's skill as a novelist has greatly improved. Confining the frame to a simple plot, Takuboku keeps the story under control both in its structure and in the manner in which he develops the plot and characters. In place of the wordy descriptions and authorial intrusions of his earlier works, Takuboku uses dialogue between the characters as the central vehicle for the development of plot and character. The novel thus becomes more dramatic and alive.

Some critics maintain that Takahashi is modeled after Futabatei Shimei, whose works Takuboku had been proofreading for publication by the *Asahi,* but whether their assumption is correct is a matter of conjecture. Regardless of the question of who the model was, it is obvious that Takuboku through his characters Takahashi and Matsunaga is presenting to the reader the profound disturbance of modern man, particularly that of the intellectual in the Meiji era, an age of turbulence and confusion caused by the inrush of new ideas from abroad.

Matsunaga represents the individual attracted to the standard designators of modernity, the things of the West, only to be lost in them. Takuboku obviously wanted to have him represent a generation who, notwithstanding its infatuation with the West, had not yet developed the capacity to fit the items of an alien culture into the unaltered framework of the old. Takahashi says about Matsunaga: "Matsunaga chose oil painting over Japanese painting; in other words, he had been wandering between the two poles. This dilemma is not only Matsunaga's; it is the problem of the whole of Meiji culture" (III, 397). In short, the dilemma in which Matsunaga has been trapped is that of the new generation of Meiji Japan who suffer from their choice of the new in a society in which the old maintains a stronger claim.

While Matsunaga personifies one aspect of modern Japan, Takahashi represents another: the lonely cry of the modern intellectual alienated from society because of his bent for self-scrutiny. Takahashi has deep within himself felt that the modern individual is a victim of his own self-awareness; it is no longer possible for him to find his identity through his relations with others in the traditional social structure. Takahashi's agony comes from this existential quest for self-identity. Further, fully realizing the danger of excessive self-examination, he devotes himself to Matsunaga's welfare, not only for Matsunaga's sake but also to liberate himself from his own self-preoccupation. After Matsunaga leaves, Takahashi next finds his release in watching movies. Takuboku's vision of modern man as shown in the characterization of Takahashi is a vision shared by many of the later generation of twentieth century writers. Examined in this light, *Our Gang and He* is ahead of its time; it is one of the earliest novels dealing with an existential inquiry into man's identity in the modern world and holds indeed a unique place in the history of modern Japanese literature.

At no time has Takuboku been regarded as a novelist of any significance. His works surely bear no comparison with those of contemporary masters of the genre, Mori Ōgai, Shimazaki Tōson and Natsume Sōseki. However, the novels do arouse interest among some Takuboku critics, particularly Kubokawa and Odagiri; even in their imperfection a certain uniqueness is apparent. Revealed in such works as *The Hospital Window*, *The Shadow of a Bird* and *Our Gang and He* is Takuboku's attempt at creating a new type of novel even when he is trying to write something in the vein of a literary movement that inspired his imagination. He is forever ahead of his time, pushing beyond the limitations of a movement to which many of his contemporaries are content to confine themselves. Furthermore, in evaluating Takuboku's novels, one needs to criticize them in a wide perspective; though taken as a whole they do not hold a significant place in the history of the modern Japanese novel, Takuboku's efforts to become a novelist gave birth to a valuable byproduct which ironically decided his fame and established his place as an important literary figure of the late Meiji era. Through his work on the novels, Takuboku's inborn skill at describing the world of heart and mind was pruned and shaped to blossom in his delicate capsule world of the tanka.

CHAPTER 5

Songs of the Heart

TAKUBOKU'S literary reputation rests first and last upon his tanka. It was through tanka written while still a student at Morioka Middle School that he was initiated into the literary world. But the tanka of his school days, though they demonstrated dexterity in imitating the Romantic school of tanka, particularly the style of Yosano Akiko, lacked originality. As might be expected of a fledgling poet the subjects he dealt with were conventional and the language, heavily dependent on traditional poetic diction, is rather affected. Takuboku's tanka composed before 1908, in short, have little literary value—as Akiko's husband, Tekkan, immediately saw. The works that have made Takuboku famous as a revolutionary poet of unique style are the tanka written between 1908 and 1911, those which were published in *A Handful of Sand* and *Sad Toys*. The evaluation of Takuboku's tanka in this chapter is therefore restricted to these two familiar collections.

Since Takuboku's first desire was to become a novelist, he did not devote himself seriously to writing tanka even after 1908, when his interest in poetry revived somewhat. Essentially the tanka were to Takuboku merely a means of releasing the frustration that developed from his lack of success as a novelist. As he remarked in his diary:

> . . . I wanted to write novels. And I tried to write them, but only to fail. Then in abusing the tanka form I found the sort of pleasure that a husband defeated in a quarrel with his wife would find in scolding and hurting a child for no reason." (IV, 211)

Feeling completely controlled by his circumstances, Takuboku found in the tanka something which *he* could control:

At the present time all that I can change freely is the position of the clock on the desk, the ink-stone box or the ink bottle and the tanka—in short, objects of very little value. I do not know how to handle the various things that inconvenience me and bring pain to my heart. . . . Turning my eyes, I caught sight of a toy, lying, as if dead, on the floor, abandoned. Tanka are my sad toys." (IV, 294–95)

To Takuboku, then, who had other literary goals, tanka were things of no practical value but were rather like "toys," providing him with brief moments of recreation and relaxation; for him, "the effect of writing tanka is no more than the effect of smoking a cigarette" (V, 299).

These statements seem to suggest that Takuboku completely disregarded the value of the tanka form. Yet that he continued to write many between 1908 and 1911 clearly indicates that he did find some meaning in composing them. Some of his letters and essays written in these years show that he believed that each moment of his life contained a valuable eternal quality and that certain emotions felt intensely in that moment could not be expressed in any way other than in tanka. While maintaining a more or less negative opinion on the status of the tanka, Takuboku did come to some appreciation of its worth as he shows in "A Dialogue Between an Egoist and His Friend," written in 1910: "A moment of life, once it is gone, never returns. I have a strong attachment to it; I do not want it to escape. In order to express that dear moment, I have found that the tanka, small in form and not requiring much trouble, is most convenient. That we have the poetic form called tanka is one of the few happinesses we Japanese have" (IV, 284). He also says in "Various Things about Poetry" written in the same year as "A Dialogue Between an Egoist and His Friend": "As long as we have a strong love for the moment that appears and disappears every second in our hearts in the midst of our busy life, the tanka will not die away. Even if the present thirty-one syllable form is changed to forty-one or even fifty-one, the tanka itself will not disappear. Therefore through it we can gratify these hearts of ours that cherish each moment of life" (IV, 294). These convictions led Takuboku to think seriously of the possibility of getting his tanka published in book form in 1910.

Takuboku's unique style did not come from a vacuum. It is the product of intense discipline as a writer in every literary genre except the drama. During his nearly five-year period (1903–1908) of training as an essayist, a poet and a novelist, the basic groundwork necessary for the creation of his tanka was laid. His keen observation of every detail of his life, his inborn gift for descriptive writing and his honesty in dealing with his inner life, all qualities essential for creating the kind of tanka he wrote, were developed in this five-year span.

I   A Handful of Sand

In early April of 1910, in an attempt to have his first collection of tanka published, Takuboku carefully selected 255 out of some 400 of his recent compositions. Although the first publisher he approached turned him down, the second, Nishimura Yōkichi, himself a tanka poet who was personally interested in Takuboku, accepted the manuscript. When an agreement between them was reached in October of the same year, the number of tanka to be included had increased to about 400. It is significant that Takuboku selected tanka for the collection only from among those written between June 23, 1908, and August 4, 1910. Takuboku's selection is a natural consequence of the change in his poetic sensibility about which he had in "From Yumi-chō" remarked.[1] The hackneyed Romantic sentiment of his early tanka was incompatible with his present down-to-earth tastes. It is apparent that Takuboku was aware that in the tanka composed in 1908 he had begun to develop a style of his own, one most suited to his poetic sensibility.

The title Takuboku first proposed for the collection was *After Work*, a title indicative of his attitude toward tanka, and all the tanka were written as one-line poems. But immediately after the manuscript was accepted for publication, Takuboku removed for further revision thirty to forty tanka and added seventy to eighty more. Then, obviously inspired by Toki Aika's *Tears and Laughter* (1910), a collection of tanka written in *rōmaji* and in three-line verse form, Takuboku divided each of his tanka into three lines and changed the title to *A Handful of Sand*. In the meantime, when Takuboku's infant son, born on October 4, died only twenty-three days after birth, the bereaved father added eight pieces in memory of the boy. The total number of tanka in *A Handful of Sand* in its final form reached 551, eighty-three percent of them written in 1910.[2]

The collection is comprised of five sections, each having a title put by Takuboku himself. The title of each section and the number of tanka in it are as follows: "Love Songs to Myself," 151; "Smoke" (1), 47; "Smoke" (2), 54; "The Good Feel of the Autumn Wind," 51; "Unforgettable People" (1), 111; "Unforgettable People" (2), 22; and "When I Pull Off My Glove," 115. From the standpoint of its subject matter and the number of tanka it contained, the first section was obviously to Takuboku the most important part of the collection.

A. *"Love Songs to Myself"*

The tanka included in "Love Songs to Myself" give us an account of this "self" in its struggle with hardship. Takuboku sings of poverty and of family life made difficult by privation, of the frustration of his ambitions, of despair and of loneliness. The songs are a journal of his everyday life kept with sincerity and candor. Consideration of these problems could have made the poet complacent with self-pity, and the tanka could have been no more than a toy to play with to comfort himself. Takuboku, however, overcame the temptation to self-indulge, and instead used the tanka as a means of mental discipline through which he learned how to objectify and govern his powerful emotions.

The subjects Takuboku treats are those such as arouse strong passions, yet the reader is struck by the plain language and simple style of his poetry. This simplicity leaves an impression that the tanka have been composed effortlessly; ironically, it is precisely because of this naturalness of style that critics have given little attention to the evaluation of Takuboku as an artist. This unaffected simplicity, however, is the result of a conscious effort to elevate his private powerful emotions into art. Such poignant feelings as loneliness and despair are crystallized when transformed into tanka. Through the tanka the reader can enter a carefully designed world and catch a glimpse of Takuboku in the latter's endeavor to preserve human dignity in the midst of the wretchedness of life. This is not to say that all the poems in *A Handful of Sand* display masterful artistic control, but there is ample evidence of Takuboku's accomplishment as an artist. While discussing the themes dealt with in the first section, let us examine some of the devices Takuboku uses to achieve this artistic wholeness.

First of all, the tanka concerned with loneliness include the following:

nan to naku kisha ni noritaku
   omoishi nomi
kisha o orishi ni
yuku tokoro nashi

just wanted to ride the train
got off
no place to go

akiya ni iri
tabako nomitaru koto ariki
aware tada hitori itaki bakarini

I've entered an empty house
and smoked there
just wanting to be alone

naniganashi ni
sabishiku nareba dete aruku
   otoko to narite
mitsuki nimo nareri

for no reason
I've begun taking walks
   when lonely
for three months now

hibon naru hito no gotoku ni
   furumaeru
nochi no sabishisa wa
nani nika taguemu[3]

the loneliness
after acting like
   somebody special
with what can I compare it?

These lines may on the surface appear to be no more than direct statements about the poet's inner feelings with little literary polish. Yet a careful reading will reveal that Takuboku has worked diligently to control the tone of each poem through use of irony. Each tanka begins with a description of a concrete dramatic situation: "riding a train," "entering an empty house," "walking out alone," "acting like a genius." By involving himself in action, Takuboku tries to overcome feelings tormenting him. Yet the irony is that the very action he engages in to alleviate his loneliness only intensifies the feeling. This irony keeps the tanka from becoming overtly sentimental.

Two more tanka similar to the one cited above are:

Asakusa no yo no nigiwai ni
magire iri
magire idekishi sabishiki kokoro

the gaiety of Asakusa's
   evening crowd
winding in, winding out
a lonely heart

komiaeru densha no sumi ni
chijikomaru
yūbe yūbe no wareno itoshisa

in the corner of a crowded train
curl myself up
alone evening after evening

Here again Takuboku presents vivid dramatic situations. In the first tanka one can easily see the poet attempting to mingle with the crowd, yet as the repetition of "wind" [*magire*]—wind in, wind out—suggests, he remains conscious of his alienation from the others. The repetition also suggests that the poet is making a repeated effort to feel at one with the crowd, but in vain. The noun ending—"*sabishiki kokoro*," the lonely heart—further intensifies the feeling that his isolated heart remains desolate. Through the juxtaposition of the liveliness and gaiety of this popular amusement quarter of Tokyo with the solitary feeling of the poet, and through the repetition of a word which brings alive the movement of the crowd and the individual winding in and out of it, Takuboku has preserved the poetic quality of the tanka in spite of such a potentially sentimental phrase as "the lonely heart."

In the second tanka quoted above Takuboku exhibits his accomplished mastery in creating a concrete image in only a few words. By using the word "*chijikomu*" ("to crouch") he immediately points out to us an alienated lonely soul, crouching in the corner of a streetcar like a frightened animal. The sense of isolation and helplessness the poet feels is thus at once relayed to the reader through the vividness of the image condensed in one word. The repetition of the word "*yūbe*" ("evening") in the last line also serves to intensify these feelings: the poet experiences the same feeling evening after evening, probably on his way home from work. Furthermore, the repetitious use of the word sharpens the impression of the poet sitting helpless, carried along by the streetcar. Also implied is the idea that not only the crowd but the streetcar as well is indifferent to the poet's feelings and that his loneliness lasts as long and as far as the streetcar runs.

Along with the skillful use of vivid description Takuboku successfully manipulates simile as a means of controlling the tone of the tanka. Two tanka stand out:

izuku yaramu kasukani mushi no
   nakugotoki
kokorobososa o
kyō mo oboyuru

like the faint chirping
   of insects
the forlornness
I feel it again today

kokoro yori kyō wa nigesareri
yamai aru kemono no gotoki
fuhei nigesareri

today they fled away
   from my heart
like a sick beast
complaints fled away

In the first example, while stressing the fact that *"kokorobososa"* ("a forlorn feeling") is a recurrently experienced feeling he successfully reduces by transmitting into the impersonal loneliness conveyed in the chirping of an insect in an evening of late summer or early autumn. The same can be said about the second tanka. Through a simile with a concrete image—*"yamai aru kemono no gotoki"* ("like a sick beast")—the poet's personal feeling of loneliness is objectified and refined upon being removed from the subjective level to the impersonal one.

Takuboku's masterful use of simile is further demonstrated in the following tanka:

shittori to   this heavy feeling
mizu o suitaru kaimen no   like a sponge
omosa ni nitaru kokochi oboyuru   that has soaked up water
                                               quietly

naniga nashi ni   somewhere in my head
atama no naka ni gake arite   there's a kind of cliff
higoto ni tsuchi no   crumbling away
    kuzururu gotoshi

In both cases Takuboku reveals through similes a vague uncertainty. In these examples Takuboku has used what might be called extended simile: the simile, drawn out from the first line to the third line, is the principal element of the poem. This particular use of simile has a special effect. In the first work, for example, before the *"kokochi"* ("feeling"—the object likened to the wet sponge) is mentioned in the last line, the extended simile has already created a feeling of uncertain dullness in the mind of the reader. He can therefore respond naturally to what the poet tries to convey when he identifies it through the word *"kokochi"*; by that time the reader has the same feeling. The second example is comprised entirely of a simile. What is compared with the crumbling cliff is left vague, and this ambiguous use of simile has left room for varied readings of the tanka. The feeling of life slipping away is brought by the image into focus.

Tabukoku's achievement as a tanka poet is thus best shown by his ability to transmute personal feeling into concrete image without loss of his subjectivity. As is shown in the examples above,

Takuboku lets the described situation recreate his private feelings without a direct intrusion of explicit sentimentality. The secret of his success lies in his ability to produce vivid images, familiar to any reader, which function as a vehicle to convey the particular feelings he has.

The chief cause of Takuboku's acute sense of loneliness was excessive self-consciousness. Despite the fact that he was blessed with good friends who showed their faith in him by their generous financial aid, for the most part he avoided people. While lending a sympathetic ear to others' problems, he seldom discussed his own; his pride prevented him from letting out his private feelings. This is the reverse side of his tendency to dramatize himself, shown particularly in his novels. Yet his exaggeration is simply a mask for the true feeling behind it. His inner struggle was a conflict known only to himself, rooted in his excessive self-criticism. Writing tanka provided him with a time and place for meditation and confession and a channel through which to release his pent up feelings. Brief though they were, the hours spent composing tanka were hours of wholeness, of being completely himself, hours of independence and self-discipline. Therefore the tanka of self-awareness give us special insight into the poet's mind. It must have been painful for Takuboku to write such tanka, and he could compose only a few of them:

kanashiki wa	how sad a man
akunaki riko no ichinen o	unable to control
moteamashitaru otoko ni arikeri	his own selfishness
kokoro yoku	want to try praising others
hito o homete mitaku narini keri	with my whole heart
riko no kokoro ni umeru sabishisa	lonely with my own selfishness
hetsurai o kikeba	at flattery
haradatsu waga kokoro	my heart grows angry
amari ni ware o	sad to know one's self
shiru ga kanashiki	too well

These tanka are plain statements of self-loathing. Takuboku is fully aware of his self-centeredness and his desire for praise; but it is the frank outpouring of such feelings that makes these works forceful. In another tanka he expresses his longing to become a person of carefree spirit:

sore mo yoshi kore mo yoshi	"this is ok. that's ok, too."
to te aru hito no	that lightheartedness
sono kigarusa o	I wish I had it
hoshiku naritari	

Whether this lightheartedness is that of a person who has never thought seriously about life or that of a saint who has achieved a detachment from worldly affairs is left to the reader to decide.

As in the tanka discussed on the preceding pages, so too in these tanka of introspection, is Takuboku at his best when projecting his feelings in a concrete image, as in the following example:

michibata ni inu	by the side of the road
naganaga to akubishinu	a dog yawns lazily
ware mo maneshinu	out of envy I imitate him
urayamashisa ni	

In this tanka, form and content are in perfect harmony. Takuboku shows varying degrees of emphasis by the length of each line with the focal point of the tanka condensed in the final line. We have the effect of the poet using a zoom lens. In the first long line (5-7-5 syllables) we have a wide view of the roadside, the dog and its leisurely yawn. The dog is free of anxiety, self-consciousness and concern for the opinion of others. The second line (seven syllables) shows us the poet imitating the dog. But, as the line is shorter than the first line, the implication is that the poet's yawn is also shorter, that checked by selfconsciousness he cannot yawn with the complete abandon of the dog. The third line brings the focus finally to rest on the mind of the poet and his motive for attempting to imitate the dog. Thus Takuboku takes us from the external situation to the internal world of his own consciousness, from which arise anxieties that do not allow him even one carefree moment. Furthermore, he knows well that an envious imitator is not an independent, self-sufficient person.

Not only loneliness but also poverty placed severe restrictions on Takuboku's freedom. It is apparent that he tried to come to grips with this problem, too, by bringing it under the discipline of meter. The majority of the tanka dealing with poverty, it must be admitted, are not good ones, but the feeling expressed in them is genuine:

| nanigoto mo kane kane to warai | money is everything, |
| sukoshi hete | I say laughing |

matamo niwakani fuhei tsunoriku

soon again
a wave of discontent

tomo yo sawa
kojiki no iyashisa
   itou nakare
uetaru toki wa ware mo
   shikari ki

o my friend
do not despise the beggar
I was like that
   when I was hungry

atarashiki inku no nioi
sen nukeba
uetaru hara ni shimu ga
   kanashi mo

the scent of fresh ink
when I uncap the bottle
sinks into my empty stomach
   with sadness

kagamiya no mae ni kite
futo odorokinu
misuborashige ni ayumu
   monokamo

in front of a mirror shop
I stopped a moment, stunned
a wretched-looking passer-by

Here again we have simple presentations of scenes from everyday life—conversations with friends, a beggar on the street, a new bottle of ink, a glimpse of himself in a mirror—all commonplace images set forth in unaffected language. Yet it is Takuboku's honesty in his description of concrete situations that has maintained the poetic quality in each of the works. Take the last two tanka, for example. In the first of the two, the plain portrayal of the gesture of opening the lid of a bottle of ink, which he has apparently bought in spite of being short of money, makes the tanka dramatic. By using a noun phrase in the first line, Takuboku lets the scent of the new ink float in the air waiting, so to speak, for the moment to enter into the empty stomach of the poet. The movement of the odor is suggested by the second line, which from a logical point of view should be in the first line. Takuboku has intentionally reversed the order of presentation to stress the severity of hunger, the result of poverty, which produces a sense of hopelessness. It is ironical that the new ink he has purchased to relieve his poverty by producing something to sell has only reminded him of his adversity. In the last tanka Takuboku sketches the effects of poverty multiplied by reflection in a mirror. The poet catches sight of his own wretchedness: the reflection of his external appearance. Not only is the person wretched, the reflection also is wretched, so that the effects of poverty are multiplied. The image of his wretched appearance gives him a sense of shock, which also is reflected. Without depending on metaphor or simile, Takuboku has succeeded in conveying a feeling of defenselessness, of being taken by surprise, and the doubling of the effect through reflection in the mirror gives a sense of a further rapid encroachment of poverty. The situation he describes, that of catching a chance glimpse of one's self in a mirror, is one that evokes an immediate response in the reader.

Peculiarly enough, though in his prose Takuboku had little to say about his family life, in the tanka he expresses his feelings about it freely, mostly of the burden it is to him:

ame fureba	it's raining, and everybody
waga ie no hito tare mo tare mo	everybody in my house
shizumeru kao su	wears a melancholy face
ame hareyo kashi	rain, go away

This tanka brings us the gloom of a rainy day made gloomier by the fact that not one member of the household *("tare mo tare mo")* can brighten it with a cheerful spirit. Takuboku does not have to spell out the fact that "rain" for him is also the rain of misfortune in his life, which none of the family helps to alleviate. He can only pray for the rain to go away. Nor does his home life give to Takuboku the relaxation he needs at the end of a hard day at work:

yoake made asobite kurasu	want a place to play till morning
basho ga hoshi	thoughts of home
ie o omoeba	chill the heart
kokoro tsumetashi	

The word *"asobu,"* here translated "play," can also mean "do nothing," so the poet is not necessarily thinking of an evening in a geisha house, though that is one possible reading; he is expressing also a simple need for rest, for some release from responsibility which he does not on his return home find. The obvious meaning of *"kokoro tsumetashi"* is that the heart of the poet freezes up when he thinks of his home; but there is also the implication that when he thinks of his home he thinks of cold hearts, namely, people who have little sympathy for him. Family life then, ironically, is a kind of death:

hito mina ga ie o motsu chō	how sad to have a family
kanashimi yo	like entering the grave
haka ni iru gotoku	coming home to sleep
kaerite nemuru	

Takuboku's frustration with his private life is further illustrated in a group of tanka that treat his daily work:

hatarakedo	I work and work
hatarakedo nao waga kurashi	but my life still
rakuni narazari	gets no better
jitto te o miru	I stare at my hands
kokoro yoku	I want work
ware ni hataraku shigoto are	that I can throw myself into
sore o shitogete shinamu to omou	and do it and die
kono tsugi no yasumi ni	"my next holiday I'll
ichinichi netemimu to	sleep all day"
omoi sugoshinu	while thinking this
mitose kono kata	three years have passed

The Takuboku portrayed in these tanka appears almost as a hero in a Naturalistic novel, struggling to survive in the face of a hostile environment. The first one, one of the best known of all his tanka, is often read as a reflection of Takuboku's socialistic as well as Naturalistic view of life. But Takuboku wrote his philosophies in prose: the tanka is no more nor less than a poignant presentation of his feelings concerning his personal life and should be read in the same context of such tanka as the other two quoted above. The struggle has brought him nothing: his hard work has not enabled him to enjoy any of the amenities of life; the reader receives the impression that the hands the poet is looking at are empty and his life is empty as well. Even the work itself, as the second tanka shows, is not satisfying; and the poet longs for some work that is challenging and worthy of his effort, to give significance to his life so that he can die satisfied. In the third tanka Takuboku tells us that the moments of leisure as well are out of his control: three years have passed without his having spent one holiday the way he wants to. The three years seem like an eternity. The poet's mention of the passing of three years gives the impression that his whole life will pass in just this way. Takuboku's striving for a sense of satisfaction and fulfillment in his work is all the more intense because he had had a taste of it:

kokoroyoki tsukare narukana	the good tired feeling
iki mo tsukazu	that comes after working hard
shigoto o shitaru nochi no	without even taking a break
kono tsukare	
nanigoto mo omou kotonaku	thinking of nothing else
isogashiku	too busy to think
kuraseshi hito hi o	that day I don't want
wasureji to omou	to forget

But the awareness that his situation is not going to improve drives him to restlessness and irritation:

me no mae no kashizara nado o	so irritated
karikari to kamite mitaku narinu	I even want to bite the cake
modokashiki kana	plate
	sitting in front of me

to mental exhaustion:

ito kuraki	feeling as if my heart
ana ni kokoro o suwareyuku	were sucked
gotoku omoite	into a very dark hole
tsukarete nemuru	I sleep exhausted

to anxiety:

futo fukaki osore o oboe	seized by a sudden deep fear
jitto shite	I sit still
yagate shizukani	then quietly grope around
heso o masaguru	my navel

and to thoughts of death:

takaki yori tobioriru gotoki	jump from a high place
kokoro mote	isn't there a way like that
kono isshō o	to end this life?
owaru sube naki ka	

shinukoto o
jiyaku o nomu ga gotoku nimo
    ware wa omoeri
kokoro itameba

death is like
taking a pet remedy
thus my painful heart
    makes me feel

nanimo kamo yukusue no koto
    miyuru gotoki
kono kanashimi wa
nugui aezumo

like seeing my whole future
this sadness
cannot be wiped away

shinitakute naranu toki ari
habakari ni hitome o sakete
kowaki kao suru

sometimes I long to die
avoiding people's eyes
I make fierce faces
    in the lavatory

shine shine to onore o ikari
modashi taru
kokoro no soko no
    kuraki munashisa

die! die! I shout at myself
then silence
in the depths of the heart
    a dark emptiness

His dejection has brought him to the verge of self-destruction. One can imagine that the discipline of putting his intense emotions under control in this restrictive thirty-one syllable verse form helped him preserve the strength of will necessary to avoid succumbing to the wish for death.

The tanka relating to Takuboku's private life include songs about his parents. Though unintentional on their part, they became one of the heaviest burdens Takuboku had to bear. Although, reasonably enough, he longed to be free of his heavy responsibilities, there is no indication that Takuboku felt any resentment toward his parents. He rather shows understanding, compassion and genuine filial devotion:

tawamure ni haha o seoite
sono amari karoki ni nakite
sanpo ayumazu

shouldered Mother just for fun
she was so light
I stopped in my tracks weeping

hokage naki shitsu ni ware ari
chichi to haha
kabe no naka yori
    tsue tsukite izu

I sit in a room
with no flicker of light
father and mother
walk out of the wall
    leaning on sticks

The first, though one of Takuboku's best known tanka, from an artistic point of view is inferior to the second. In the first, the situation described is a bit theatrical and the poet's emotion is exaggerated. The overtly sentimental word *"nakite"* ("weeping") mars the otherwise carefully controlled poem. Takuboku skillfully shifts the tone from the cheerfulness of the first line to the sadness of the last, but at a crucial point he slips into banal sentimentalism. The second tanka, on the other hand, is refined and one of the best tanka in this collection. Takuboku describes a situation which brings out his feelings toward his parents. The reader is led into the lonely atmosphere of a dark room where the poet sits alone. The feeling of intimacy with his parents, and awareness of their spiritual presence, is brought out forcefully in the image of their coming out of the wall. But as they are aged and dependent, leaning on sticks, the reader feels, too, the poet's awareness of his failure as their son to provide for their welfare. As clearly shown in this work again, Takuboku's mastery of tanka is best demonstrated when he merely presents or narrates a situation while himself remaining in the background. This does not mean that his personal feelings are suppressed; on the contrary, the dramatic situation he creates provides a vivid and effective means for projecting his feelings. This device is an extension of that of using a concrete image as a channel for expressing his private world of emotion.

In the midst of the series of tanka dealing for the most part with his inner torment, Takuboku brought together in the section of "Love Songs to Myself" a group of tanka of a different tone. This group celebrates, through accomplished manipulation of images, moments when he experienced quiet joy and peace of mind:

mare ni aru
kono tairanaru kokoro niwa
tokei no naru mo omoshiroku kiku

how seldom it is
with a quiet heart
I enjoy the chiming
    of the clock

tokaku shite ie o izureba
nikkō no atatakasa ari
iki fukaku suu

busy with this and that
    I step outside
feeling the warmth of the sun
I take a deep breath

ōdoka no kokoro kitareri
aruku nimo

this expansive feeling
even in walking

hara ni chikara no tamaru ga gotoshi	I feel strong inside
arutoki no ware no kokoro o yakitate no pan ni nitari to omoi kerukana	sometimes my heart is like a loaf of bread just baked in the oven
aruhi no koto heya no shōji o harikaenu sono hi wa sore nite kokoro nagomiki	the day I changed the paper on the shoji I felt good all day long
hate mo mienu masugu no machi o ayumu gotoki kokoro o kyō wa mochietaru kana	like walking on a straight road with no end in sight had that good feeling today

ryō no gotoku munashiki
  sora ni odori idete
kieyuku kemuri
mireba akanaku
	like a dragon the smoke
	  dances in the sky
	and disappears
	never tire of watching it

These tanka are valuable evidence that the melancholy poet had his cheerful side also; indeed, the moments of pleasure may have been all the more intense because they came so rarely. All of the poems give us simple scenes of simple pleasures: hearing the clock strike, enjoying the sunshine, taking a walk, delighting in the new paper on the shoji that gives a feeling of freshness to the room. Images used in these tanka give the warm feeling of a sunny spring day. Particularly such images as "fresh baked bread," "smoke rising like a dragon" and "the quiet heart," characteristically Takuboku's, do much to brighten this otherwise gloomy section.

"Love Songs to Myself" indeed sings of Takuboku's inner life, revealing the various moods experienced by his sensitive and delicate mind. It is easy to understand why he placed it at the beginning of *A Handful of Sand.*

B. *"Smoke"*

The second section of *A Handful of Sand* is divided into two parts, "Smoke" (1) and (2), dealing respectively with Takuboku's nostalgia for his childhood and for his childhood home. The subject has offered him an opportunity to objectify himself, and as a result the tone of the section is on the whole much lighter and livelier than that of the first section examined above, as represented by the following tanka:

ameuri no charumera kikeba	with the candy seller's flute
ushinaishi	returns
osanaki kokoro hiroeru gotoshi	my lost childhood

Takuboku's imagination flows freely as his memories of the past momentarily emancipate him from morbid preoccupation with himself and his present unhappiness. The memories of childhood, now too soon lost, are to the heart of Takuboku in the arid desert of his adult life in the city an oasis, so to speak.

Reminiscing of the days gone by, particularly childhood and life in the country, holds a special meaning for Takuboku, as he has remarked elsewhere:

People often say that to reminisce of the days gone by is unmanly and spiritless, the courage to move forward emasculated. Nonetheless, for us who are born into a world of retrogression to recall the golden age long gone gives rise to new strength, new faith and new hope for the days to come. If we, born in this age, cannot reminisce of the past, there will be left with us nothing but despair and suicide, and the assurance that comes from our faith in the ideal, which is our whole life, will all disappear like foam on the surface of water. (V, 86–87)

There is some exaggeration in Takuboku's statement, particularly in the use of such an expression as "the golden age," a notion foreign to Japanese culture; but undoubtedly he sensed in the memory of the past a value comparable to the glory of a golden age when gods and mortals could live together in harmony. This memory of the past makes the present wretched life easier to endure by bringing it a touch of beauty and by bringing to the poet not only comfort and peace of mind but hopes and dreams as well. Hope is necessary for survival in the city because "industrialized society," impersonal machinelike society, threatens to deprive an individual of his basic humanity, which only life in the country seems to nourish and preserve. As we have seen in Chapter 3, Takuboku felt keenly the impersonality and dehumanization, the junglelike atmosphere of life in the city: "Sharpened senses and paralyzed morality are the two products of city life. They [city migrants] have lost not only their homes but their consciences as well—not just their nostalgia for the country but for all that should be yearned for" (IV, 286). To put it differently, either in the form of memories of his childhood or in the form of memories of his country home, recollecting the past renders it possible for him to restore the basic elements that make him most human—love, compassion, gratitude and kindness—and to maintain hope and a sense of order and balance that would enable him to live fully even in his present confined circumstances. Takuboku attempts to find this sense of fullness in singing of the memory of the past with its shadow cast far into the present and future. It is the shadow of innocence and purity, which points to the possibility of a better, more meaningful life. Therefore for Takuboku nostalgia for the past is not so much a reflection of sentimentality or despair regarding his present life as an attempt to preserve his own integrity in the midst of present wretchedness, aggravated by the indifference of city society to the private feelings of the individual. However, one cannot deny that Takuboku is using thoughts of the past as a means of temporary escape from the present and that the infant world recaptured in memory is somewhat romantically idealized. But the flight is a necessary one for him to reevaluate his life and restore his confidence in his ability to come to grips with adversity. Viewed in this light, Takuboku's concept of the value of memory is almost Wordsworthian: memory enables him not only to recapture the past but also to discover the potential of new life.

The majority of the forty-seven tanka constituting "Smoke" (1) are concerned with Takuboku's memory of childhood, its sweetness and delight. Childhood and youth are full of such blessings as innocence, naturalness, joy and freedom from care:

Kozukata no oshiro no kusa ni
  nekorobite
sora ni suwareshi
jūgo no kokoro
	stretched out on the grass
	  of Kozukata Castle
	sucked up into the wide sky
	my fifteenth summer

kyōshitsu no mado yori nigete
tada hitori
kano shiroato ni
  ne ni yukishi kana
	slipping out the window
	  of the classroom
	all alone
	go to take a nap at the castle

hana chireba mazu hitosaki ni shiro no fuku kite ie izuru ware nite arishika	when the cherry blossoms fell I was the first to go out in summer clothes
yoru netemo kuchibue fukinu kuchibue wa jūgo no ware no uta ni shi arikeri	whistling in bed at night whistling my own song a song of my fifteenth year

hareshi sora aogeba itsumo
kuchibue o fukitaku narite
fukite asobiki

looking up at a clear sky
makes me want to whistle
I used to enjoy doing that

yoku shikaru shi ariki
hige no nitaru yori
    yagi to nazukete
kuchimane mo shiki

the teacher who scolded us
    a lot
we called him "goat" because
    of his beard
and mimicked the way he talked

The cares and anxieties of adult life, on the other hand, have
supplanted these attributes of childhood which enabled him to enjoy life with spontaneity. The grown man is in a "prison-house," to
use Wordsworth's phrase, of social responsibilities.

Among the tanka dealing with his youth Takuboku included three
pieces that attract special attention. Unlike the majority of tanka in
this section these three have a rather melancholy restrained tone,
for they deal with one of life's ironies. A very special pleasure of his
youth became the cause of his premature aging:

kanashimi to iwaba yūbeki
mono no aji
ware no nameshi wa
    amarini hayakari

call this sorrow
the flavor of something
tasted too soon

shiroato no
ishi ni koshikake
kinsei no konomi o hitori
    ajiwaishi koto

among the castle ruins
on a stone, alone
I flavored forbidden fruit

sakinjite koi no amasa to
kanashisa o shirishi warenari
sakinjite oyu

too young I knew
love's sweets and pain
too young grew old

One can easily identify what Takuboku means by "the flavor of
something" and "forbidden fruit." The allusion to "forbidden fruit,"
obviously derived from the book of *Genesis*, fits in well with what he
wants to say in these three tanka: Takuboku tasted at once the
sweetness of love and the bitterness of life too soon. In other words,
he experienced "the fall" from a state of innocence to a state of
experience, a state which to Takuboku meant the assumption of
responsibilities as husband, father and son. Judging from the tone of
all three tanka quoted above, one can sense that Takuboku regrets,
if not his marrriage itself, the fact that he was married too soon, a

decision which forced an early maturity. The imagery of tasting the forbidden fruit is borrowed and in that sense it is artificial; but by bringing it into a personal context Takuboku successfully salvaged the tanka from sounding merely contrived.

Another object of Takuboku's reminiscence as valuable as scenes from his childhood and youth is the village of Shibutami, where he grew up, its natural beauty and the people who lived there. It is these reminiscences which make up the second part of "Smoke." As one of his tanka, quoted in Chapter 1, reads

ishi o mote owaruru gotoku	as if driven out by stoning
furusato o ideshi kanashimi	I left the village
kiyuru toki nashi	that sorrow never fades away

not all memories of Shibutami are pleasant. The passing of the years, however, casts a romantic glow over the village; and in Takuboku's imagination Shibutami is transformed into an ideal realm of peace and happiness. It thus becomes associated in Takuboku's mind with his image of utopia.[4] Thinking of his childhood home, like conceiving an image of utopia, provides him with moments of joy and freedom from worldly concerns for which he longs all the more as his hardships increase:

furusato no yama ni mukaite	the mountains of home
yūkoto nashi	no words to describe
furusato no yama wa arigataki kana	the blessed sight
yamai aru kemono no gotoki	irritable as a sick animal
waga kokoro	my heart
furusato no koto kikeba otonashi	hearing of home becomes calm
futo omou	suddenly realized
furusato ni ite higoto kikishi suzume no naku o	the sparrows I heard every day at home
mitose kikazari	I haven't heard for three years
bareisho no usu-murasaki no hana ni furu	in the Tokyo rain I recall the rain falling
ame o omoeri	on purple potato flowers
miyako no ame ni	

Even if Takuboku had written nothing else, the first tanka in the above group would have insured a permanent place for him in Japanese literature and in the hearts of the Japanese people. A regular part of present junior high school Japanese literature courses, it is one of the most widely known and frequently quoted of Japanese poems. Capturing the deep attachment to home, family, old friends and native place that is a fundamental element of Japanese psychology, Takuboku's tanka strikes a sympathetic chord in the hearts of his countrymen.

Recollections of the inhabitants of the village anticipate in their vivid descriptions the tanka in the "Unforgettable People" section:

ijiwaru no daiku no ko nado mo kanashikari	the son of the bad-tempered carpenter
ikusa ni ideshi ga	he went to war
ikite kaerazu	but didn't come back alive
sake nomeba	the teacher who when drunk
katana o nukite tsuma o ou	would draw a sword
kyōshi mo ariki	and chase his wife
mura o owareki	was chased out of the village
tomo to shite asobumono naki	they had no one to play with
shōwaru no junsa no kora mo	the children of the
aware narikeri	ill-natured policeman
	what a pity!
waga tame ni	there was one
nayameru tama o shizumeyo to	who sang hymns
sanbika utau hito arishi kana	to calm my troubled spirit
waga mura ni	the young woman
hajimete Iesu Kurisuto no	who first preached the way
michi o tokitaru	of Jesus Christ
wakaki onna kana	in our village

Although the portraits themselves are unadorned, unromanticized, the succinctness of the portrayal adds a touch of pathos to the nostalgia. In these plain lines old friends and acquaintances of Takuboku indeed come alive.

While it is true that the tanka of this section by and large maintain a lightness of tone, Takuboku's awareness that moments of recalling the past, in spite of their beauty and the pleasure they bring, are after all fleeting, distills a tone of melancholy, even sadness, into the poems. The reader can sense Takuboku's ambivalence of attitude toward the value of these recollections. On the one hand is the positive aspect that memory of the past serves to preserve his basic humanity which, with its reminder that life can be better, provides him with a dream for the future. The negative aspect manifests itself when Takuboku faces up to the fact that memory can too easily become no more than a temporary flight from present responsibilities and that one must eventually return to the actual world of struggle. Takuboku's ambivalence toward these recollections is best illustrated in the title he chose for this section. Memories of his childhood and the feeling of satisfaction he experiences in reliving the past are like smoke rising from a chimney:

aozora ni kieyuku kemuri	smoke vanishing in the blue sky
sabishiku mo kieyuku kemuri	desolately vanishing smoke
ware ni shi niruka	my life is like that

and his past life is:

ito kireshi tako no gotoku ni	like a kite with a broken
wakaki hi no kokoro karokumo	string
tobisarishi kana	the dreams of my youth
	have all flown away

ishi hitotsu	like a stone
saka o kudaru ga gotoku nimo	rolling down a hill
ware kyō no hi ni itari	I have come to
tsukitaru	the present day

The tone of the whole section of "Smoke," then, is characterized by a beautiful sadness, the characteristic poetic sensibility of traditional Japanese poetry. Deeply rooted in the sentiment is the philosophical awareness of the transitory nature of beauty. Evaluated in this light the tone of melancholy beauty is a manifestation of Takuboku's pain and joy at once: the memory of his carefree childhood makes him clearly conscious of the tragic contradiction between what his life used to be and what it now actually is. Yet he must sing about the past. The moment of recollection, though brief, sheds a bright light on the otherwise dark landscape of the present: "aware waga nosutarujiya wa kin no goto kokoro ni tereri kiyoku shimirani" "like rich pure gold it shines in my heart this longing for home"

C. *"The Good Feel of the Autumn Wind"*

Forty-four of the fifty tanka that comprise the third section of *A Handful of Sand* were written in 1908, and the majority of them deal specifically with autumn, as the title of the section indicates. It should be noted that 1908 was the year when Takuboku suddenly resumed writing tanka, not yet conscious of the possible development of a style and content of his own. In short, it was Takuboku's second apprenticeship in tanka composition, the first being in his middle school days at Morioka. Simplicity of language and ease of style demonstrate increased mastery, yet the scope of the tanka is limited in that he follows the convention of waka poets whose major interest lay in objective description of the world of nature. A few examples will suffice to show Takaboku's imitations of the conventional style:

matsu no kaze
   yo hiru hibikinu
hito towanu yama no hokora no
ishi-uma no mimi ni

the wind in the pines
   day and night
whistles in the ears
   of the stone horse
at the mountain shrine
   no man visits

mizutamari
kureyuku sora to kurenai no
   himo o ukabenu
akisame no nochi

in the puddle
the sunset sky and a crimson
   spider's web floating
after an autumn rain

hatahata to kibi no ha nareru
furusato no nokiba natsukashi
akikaze fukeba

I can hear the flapping
   of the corn stalks
under the eaves of
   my old home
when the autumn wind blows

honoka naru kuchiki no kaori
soga naka no take no kaori ni
aki yaya fukashi

in the gentle scent
   of the decayed tree
the fragrance of mushrooms
deeper into autumn

shigure furu gotoki oto shite
kozutainu
hito ni yoku nishi mori no
   sarudomo

like the sound of rain falling
they fly from tree to tree
the forest monkeys
   resembling people

Suppressing his personal feelings, the poet evokes the detached impersonal loneliness of the season, a sensation powerful enough to make the reader oblivious to the poet's presence.

The danger of too closely following the convention of waka is, of course, that the work tends to be contrived, especially when the poet attempts to sing about an imaginary poetic situation. A good example illustrating the case in point is:

ao ni suku	transparent blue
kanashimi no tama ni	jewel of sadness for a pillow
makurashite	I hear the soughing of the
matsu no hibiki o	pines all night
yomosugara kiku	

The subject is trite, the language affected and spontaneity of feeling absent. Another example of affected convention is:

ametsuchi ni	in heaven and earth
waga kanashimi to gekkō	my grief and the moonlight
amaneki aki no yo to narerikeri	everywhere in the autumn night

However, the fact that Takuboku in 1911 selected these tanka for publication in spite of their demerits indicates that he could perceive in them early buds of the flowering of his own style. Even among the tanka of conventional style and subject matter, one can discern the touch of Takuboku's individuality. The following example, for instance, clearly shows Takuboku moving toward his own style: that is, a subjective portrayal of nature:

aki no sora kakuryō to shite	the autumn sky desolate
kage mo nashi	and empty
amarini sabishi	too lonely
karasu nado tobe	crow or something, fly

After describing in the first seventeen syllables the forlorn scene of the autumn sky, he unhesitatingly pours out his personal reaction. In other words, in the last half of the poem he transfers the emphasis of the tanka from an external to an internal loneliness. The violent expression of feelings in the second half damages the poetic quality of the tanka, yet the abruptness of the shift in perspective all the more intensifies the sense of loneliness within, which is contrasted with that of the vast autumn sky. The loneliness the tanka deals with is of the kind felt by an individual awakened to the question of his identity. The poet has been driven to consciousness of self by the awareness of his isolation from nature, a consciousness brought about by the impersonal atmosphere nature has created. It is this awareness of isolation which makes him cry out. This declaration of his loneliness functions therefore as a reaffirmation of his existence under the vast impersonal expanse of the autumn sky; and his call for a crow to fly is not for the sake of the sky but for himself, out of desire for fellowship with another living thing. The juxtaposition of the impersonal loneliness of the outside world and the loneliness the poet feels within him enlarges the scope of the poem: the division between man and nature is irreconcilable. Other tanka dealing with nature as a reflection of his inner feelings are:

aki no koe mazu ichihayaku
    mimi ni iru
kakaru saga motsu
kanashimu bekari
	the voice of autumn reaches
	    my ears first
	to have this kind of nature
	is sad

chichi no goto aki wa ikameshi haha no goto aki wa natsukashi ie motanu ko ni	like a father autumn is stern like a mother autumn is dear to the homeless child

In additon to the free use of his subjective feelings, another distinctive characteristic of Takuboku's style is, as we have seen above, the use of a simile that gives concreteness in description. Among the tanka in the section "The Good Feel of Autumn Wind" there are a few which for their apt similes deserve special attention:

karisome ni wasurete mo mimashi
ishidatami
haru ouru kusa ni
    umoruru ga goto
	I wish to forget even
	    for a while
	like the stone pavement
	buried in the spring grass

nagaku nagaku wasureshi tomo ni
au gotoki
yorokobi o mote mizu no
    oto kiku
	as if meeting
	a long-forgotten friend
	I listen with joy to the
	    sound of the water

aki no ame ni sakazori yasuki
    yumi no goto
konogoro
kimi no shitashimanu kana
	like an arrow easily warped
	    in the autumn rain
	these days
	you avoid me

In these three poems, by using a simile borrowed from nature, Takuboku not only adds depth to each but also contributes even a touch of humor (see particularly the first and third tanka) which moderates the seriousness of his message. These comparisons are natural and spontaneous, showing that Takuboku had an inborn gift in his use of simile, the distinctive artistic feature of the tanka in *A Handful of Sand.*

D. *"Unforgettable People"*

The individuals Takuboku sings about in the section of "Unforgettable People" represent the wide variety of people he was acquainted with. No other tanka poet wrote so extensively about his own circle of friends and acquaintances as did Takuboku. This concentration on individuals is a valuable development of an additional possibility of the tanka. The majority of the people sung about are those Takuboku came to know while he was in Hokkaido; his status as a newcomer there and the frequent separations from his family must have intensified for him relations with people in his immediate environment. At any rate, the people who were especially significant to him are immortalized in Takuboku's tanka.

Takuboku divided this section into two parts. In the first he included tanka about a variety of people in no special order and put in some tanka on nature as well. The second part, on the other hand, concentrates on only one individual. From the standpoint of Takuboku's poetic treatment of his various subjects, however, it is more revealing to take up the tanka according to the degree of personal intimacy that Takuboku enjoyed with each. For that reason we will look first at the poems about people with whom he had close relationships and then move on to tanka about people from his larger circle of acquaintances. Finally we will consider the tanka written about scenes from nature which Takuboku thought as unforgettable as people. In these tanka Takuboku is able to gain a detachment difficult to achieve in poems about human beings and human relationships.

The person of foremost importance was his friend Miyazaki Ikuu:

enshū no hima ni wazawaza	the sake drunk with my friend
kisha ni norite	who took the trouble to come
toikishi tomo to nomeru	a long way by train
sake kana	on a short leave

The description of this special occasion serves also to give a character sketch of the person who brought it about, and reveals the great value the friendship had for both of them. This tanka, therefore, by telling us what Miyazaki did, shows us the kind of person he is. His character is clearly revealed in the expression *"wazawaza"* ("took the trouble to," "went out of the way to"), which also reflects Takuboku's gratitude toward the friend who is paying a visit to him from a faraway place.

Another tanka about Miyazaki is:

ōkawa no mizu no omote o	whenever I look at the surface
mirugoto ni	of a large river
Ikuu yo	Ikuu
kimi no nayami o omou	I think of your sorrow

This tanka specifically refers to the evening of October 12, 1908, when Miyazaki and Takuboku had a long talk. Miyazaki's book, *The Sand of Hakodate: Takuboku's Tanka and I,* tells that at that time he had been wrestling with the problem "any serious youth of the day confronted,"[5] the problem of how to find meaning in life. Miyazaki was questioning the value of life, of love and of marriage, and Takuboku, a sympathetic listener, had continually borne in mind his friend's struggle. Through the image of a capacious river Takuboku shows his genuine concern for his friend: the vastness of the problem over which Miyazaki is agonizing and the depth of Takuboku's empathy.

Takuboku's best character portrayal is contained in a group of tanka about a geisha named Konatsu (or Koyakko), who brought warmth and comfort to his life in Kushiro:

Koyakko to iishi onna no	it's hard to forget
yawarakaki	even the soft ear-lobes
mimitabo nado mo	and such
wasuregata kari	of the girl Koyakko
shinitaku wa nai ka to ieba	"Have you ever wanted to die?"
kore miyo to	"Look at this," she replied
nondo no kizu o miseshi	showing the scar on her throat
onna kana	
shinubakari waga you o machite	waiting for me to be
iroiro no	dead drunk

kanashiki koto o	she whispered to my ears
sasayakishi hito	all sorts of sad things
kishikishi to samusa ni	on the floor creaking
fumeba ita kishimu	with the cold
kaeri no rōka no	as I was about to leave
fui no kuchizuke	an unexpected kiss

Takuboku's mastery of realism in describing minute details helps create a picture of her physical characteristics and, more significantly, her personality, the tender memory of which Takuboku held dear.

The second section of "Unforgettable People" consists of twenty-two tanka entirely devoted to his recollections of Tachibana Chieko, a school teacher he came to know in June, 1907. Chieko was employed at the elementary school where Takuboku started working as a part time teacher shortly after he was appointed editor of the *Crimson Medic*. Takuboku was much attracted by Chieko's refined beauty and a grace of manner that indicated her good breeding . The fire of 1907 that destroyed the school building and the headquarters of Circle of Medics, however, brought his acquaintance with Chieko to an abrupt end; he was compelled to leave Hakodate for Sapporo to take a new job. Just before leaving he gave her a copy of *Longing*. Despite the brevity of their association, it is apparent that Chieko left a strong impression on Takuboku and that he cherished her memory. Three years later after the publication of *A Handful of Sand* he sent her a copy of the book along with a postcard mentioning the fact that she had been the inspiration for this particular section of the work. Among the tanka Chieko read about herself were:

yama no ko no	as the mountain child
yama o omou ga gotoku ni mo	thinks of the mountains
kanashiki toki wa kimi o omoeri	I think of you when sad
wakarekite toshi o kasanete	the years since we parted
toshigoto ni koishiku nareru	every year the longing increases
kimi ni shi arukana	for you
kimi ni nishi sugata o	when on the streets I see
machi ni miru toki no	someone resembling you
kokoro odori o	my heart leaps
aware to omoe	feel pity for me

Ishikari no miyako no soto no
kimiga ie
ringo no hana no chirite ya aramu

at your home on the outskirts
of the capital of Ishikari
have the apple blossoms
  scattered yet?

yo no naka no akarusa nomi o
  sū gotoki
kuroki hitomi no
ima mo me ni ari

those dark eyes that look as if
they absorb only the world's
  brightness
even now I can see them

nagaki fumi
mitose no uchi ni mitabi kinu
ware no kakishi wa
  yotabi nika aramu

three times in three years
a long letter has come
I've written four times maybe

bareisho no hana saku koro to
nareri keri
kimi mo kono hana o
  sukitamauramu

potato-blossom time
has come
you, too, like these flowers,
  don't you?

One can see that the memories associated with Chieko are of a quite
different nature from those of Koyakko. From Koyakko Takuboku
retains physical details and conversations. Recollections of Chieko,
while including memories of her person, are part of a larger ideal
image, associated with the life-renewing forces of nature, with a
stability of place, with beauty, comfort and human goodness. In
Takuboku's imagination the image of Chieko has a function much
like that of his childhood home, Shibutami. The reader can recognize similarities of reference in the two groups of poems, as in the
poems about the potato flowers and the poems mentioning that
three years have passed. Both groups of poems are conspicuous for
having a predominant tone of joy and tranquility which sets them
apart from the larger body of the tanka dealing with loneliness and
suffering.

In the section "Love Songs to Myself" we find a few tanka about
Takuboku's parents; and in this section also he included three tanka
dealing with members of his family, this time his mother, wife and a
sister:

waga ato o oikite
shireru hito mo naki
hendo ni sumishi haha to
  tsuma kana

they've followed me
to this out-of-the-way place
where they know no one,
  my mother and my wife

fune ni yoite yasashiku nareru	when I think of the
imōto no me miyu	Tsugaru Strait
Tsugaru no umi o omoeba	I see my sister's eyes
	she was gentle when seasick
ko o oite	the baby on her back
yuki no fukiiru teishaba ni	in the falling snow
ware miokurishi	at the station
tsuma no mayu kana	seeing me off, my wife's
	eyebrows

As in the tanka on Chieko, these poems are not personality sketches of the individuals depicted. Takuboku describes instead memories associated with them, only this time the memories are of discomfort and privation which they as family members were compelled to share with him on coming to Hokkaido. These memories are all the more painful because their troubles, of course, did not leave them when they left Hokkaido to come to Tokyo. In Takuboku's imagination, as far as the suffering of his family is concerned, the present is merely a continuation of the past and recollections of family members serve also as reminders of the present daily struggle. Whereas other tanka in this section, including the recollections of Chieko, bring a kind of joy and serenity in their tone of gentle nostalgia, these three about the family give only a sense of heartrending helplessness. The image of journey in these tanka functions well to produce a desolate melancholy tone.

Among Takuboku's "unforgettable people" are some with whom he had only limited acquaintance or merely chance encounters. The inclusion of tanka written about these individuals from various stations in life brings an added color and richness to this section. Takuboku's appreciation of the uniqueness of each person and his ability to empathize with others discloses his profound humanity and makes these tanka full of life:

kanashimeba takaku waraiki	laughing aloud when sad
sake o mote	"Drown your troubles in wine"
mon o gesu to yū	said that older woman
toshiue no tomo	
aojiroki hō ni namida o	his pale cheeks
hikarasete	shining with tears
shi o ba katariki	he talked of death
wakaki akibito	the young merchant

toru ni taranu otoko to omoe to
  yū gotoku
yama ni iriniki
kami no gotoki tomo

as if to say "Just think of me
  as a worthless fellow"
he went into the mountains
my friend like a god

isasaka no zeni karite yukishi
waga tomo no
ushiro sugata no
  kata no yuki kana

borrowing a trifling sum
  of money
my friend is gone
the snow on his back shoulder

osoraku wa shōgai
  tsuma o mukaeji to
waraishi tomo yo
ima mo metorazu

"I'll probably never get
  married"
said my young friend
he's still single

muyamuya to
kuchi no uchi nite tōtoge no
  koto o tsubuyaku
kojiki mo ariki

there was a beggar
mumbling in his mouth
something which might be
  valuable

wakaku shite
sūnin no chichi to narishi tomo
konaki ga gotoku yoeba utaiki

the young father of several
  children
when he's drunk
he sings like a bachelor

utaugoto eki no na yobishi
nyūwa naru
wakaki ekifu no me o mo
  wasurezu

can't forget the eyes
of the mild-mannered young
  station man
who called out the station's
  name as though singing

These poems are seemingly no more than offhand descriptions of various individuals, yet one feels that the poet has a sense of the identity of the characters, each of whom is carrying the burden of life in his own way. The result is a poignancy in the sketches that makes the characters portrayed unforgettable to the reader. One might even say that Takuboku has done better in writing about these surface acquaintances than in writing about individuals with whom he was more intimate. The emotional distance and detachment rounds out his perspective and leaves more space for the workings of poetic imagination. Perhaps in these tanka we can catch a glimpse of the direction in which Takuboku might have developed had he been granted more time.

    Scattered through this section, too, are several tanka objectively describing the world of nature, completely free from human passions. In these tanka Takuboku has become a master of the nature poem, his identity completely merged in the landscape he describes:

yuki no naka	through the snow
shosho ni yane miete	roofs showing here and there
entotsu no kemuri usukumo	smoke from a chimney rises
sora ni mayoeri	thinly into the sky
tōku yori	from far away
fue naganaga to hibikasete	with a long wail of the whistle
kisha ima toaru shinrin ni iru	the train is now entering
	a forest
shirashira to kōri kagayaki	ice sparkling white
chidori naku	the plover cries
Kushiro no umi no fuyu no	the winter moon of Kushiro
tsuki kana	Bay
Sorachigawa yuki ni umorete	Sorachi River buried in snow
tori mo miezu	not a bird in sight
kishibe no hayashi ni	in the forest on the bank
hito hitori iki	one solitary person

These tanka are very much like paintings: captured by the poet's acute sensitivity, the moment of beauty is in simple language eternally preserved. The landscape portrayed here encompasses a solitary calm. This group indeed displays Takuboku's virtuosity as a poet capable of objectifying his strong feelings.

E. *"When I Pull Off My Glove"*

The last section of *A Handful of Sand* is a miscellaneous assortment of tanka, the tone of which is aptly set forth in the first tanka, from which the title is taken:

tebukuro o nugu te futo yamu	I pull off my glove and chance
nani yaramu	to pause
kokoro kasumeshi	there's something
omoide no ari	a memory flitting through
	my heart

On the whole the poetic quality of the tanka here is inferior to that of the previous sections. Let us look, however, at some that are deserving of attention.

As we have seen, one recurrent theme in Takuboku's tanka is loneliness:

mite oreba tokei tomareri	while I was looking at it
suwaruru goto	the clock stopped
kokoro wa matamo	like it just sat down
sabishisa ni yuku	I went back to loneliness
	again

In the first line *"tomareri"* (has stopped) tells us that a clock the poet had been looking at suddenly stopped. The word *"matamo"* ("again") in the final line reveals that he had been completely absorbed in its ticking, oblivious to anything else. The clock's coming to a stop thrusts the poet once more into the world of self-consciousness. The abrupt return to loneliness is pointed up sharply in these two simple words: his moment of freedom has come to an end *("tomareri")* and he must return to himself again *("matamo")*. The contrast of noise and silence creates an interesting paradox. The silence without the ticking of the clock fills the poet's mind with the noise of his own restlessness. There is a further contrast of movement and stillness. While the clock is moving the poet can sit calmly, but when the clock "sits" [*"suwaruru goto"*] then the poet must move, go [*"yuku"*] into loneliness.

One of Takuboku's frequently employed techniques, that of borrowing an image from nature to portray by contrast his own inner feelings, is used with especial skill in the following tanka:

usureyuku shōji no hikage	the thinning light on the
so o mitsutsu	shoji
kokoro itsushika kuraku	while watching it
nariyuku	my heart has darkened unawares
shiroki hasu-numa ni saku gotoku	like the white lotus blooming
kanashimi ga	in the marsh
yoi no aida ni hakkiri to uku	sadness
	floats vividly in drunkenness

In both cases the image is brilliant. In the first tanka thinning light of the setting sun is used as a metaphor for sinking feelings within the poet. In the second the vivid white of the water lily in a murky swamp represents the heart of a human being whose sorrow has been aggravated rather than reduced by the supposedly Lethean sake. The contrast between the world of nature and the world of the poet is painfully obvious. In the natural world the sun sets only to rise the following morning, but the darkening heart contains no promise of possible recovery. Similarly, the water lily's whiteness makes the swamp bright, maintaining its integrity unaffected by its surroundings. The human heart, on the other hand, is overpowered by its environment: its opening brings no light but only casts a deeper shadow. In short, there exists an unbridgeable gulf between nature, from which the poet draws his images, and the poet's heart, which the images are used to portray. The sense of sorrow is therefore doubly intense.

In contrast to this ironic juxtaposition of nature and man, one can find other poems, more in the tradition of Japanese poetry, which show the poet at one with the calm of nature:

kokoro yoku
haru no nemuri o musaboreru
me ni yawarakaki niwa no
    kusa kana

in the eyes
craving a refreshing spring
    nap
the soft garden grass

haru no yuki
Ginza no ura no sangai no
    renga-zukuri ni
yawarakani furu

on the three-storied brick
    building behind the Ginza
spring snow
softly falls

surudokumo
natsu no kitaru o
    kanji-tsutsu
ugo no koniwa no tsuchi no
    ka o kagu

feeling keenly
the coming of summer
the earth-smell of the small
    garden after rain

hito naraba oyogeru gotoki
ie-ie no takahiku no noki ni
fuyu no hi no mau

like a person swimming
on the eaves of houses
    high and low
the winter sun is dancing

Takuboku's detached and detailed description has guarded him from indulging in personal feelings.

In addition to themes already dealt with in the first four sections of *A Handful of Sand*, Takuboku included in this last section tanka inspired by two unforgettable experiences of 1910. The first event, the High Treason Incident, was of course too large a subject to be covered in tanka. What Takuboku did condense into tanka were sketches of himself with a book that had been banned by the government, and a chance meeting with the author of the same book:

akagami no hyōshi tezureshi	the banned book with
kokkin no	the worn red cover
fumi o kōri no soko ni	the day I searched for it
sagasu hi	in the bottom of the trunk
urukoto o sashitomerareshi	the autumn morning I met
hon no chosha ni	on the street
michi nite aeru aki no asa kana	the author of the book
	whose sale had been banned

The original version of the first tanka was:

akagami no hyōshi tezureshi	absorbed in reading
kokkin no sho yomi fukeri	the banned book with worn out
natsu no yo o nezu	red covers
	the sleepless autumn night

The original contains a sense of excitement aroused by the poet's violating the law in secret, yet the static description lacks the intensity and thrill that the published form brings out. Takuboku gave more life to the poem by creating in the last fourteen syllables a dramatic situation of almost fearful anticipation by bringing the spotlight to bear on the man searching for the outlawed book.

Another event of major significance for Takuboku was, of course, the birth and death of his son. On October 4, 1910, Takuboku became the father of a son, an event celebrated by the following tanka: "jūgatsu no asa no kūki ni atarashiku iki suisomeshi akanbo no ari ("in the air of an October morning an infant newly began to breathe") But his joy was not to last long. On October 27:

yoru osoku	late at night
tsutome-saki yori kaerikite	returning from work
ima shinishi chō ko o	to hold the just-dead child
dakeru kana	
futamikoe	two or three faint cries
imawa no kiwa ni kasuka ni mo	just before he died
nakishi to yū ni	hearing this brought tears
namida sasowaru	

mashiro naru daikon no ne no 　koyuru koro umarete yagate shinishi ko no ari	the white *daikon* grows fat a child was born and died
osoaki no kūki o sanshaku shihō bakari suite waga ko no shini- 　yukishi kana	the late autumn air of one small room breathing only this my child has gone
shinishi ko no mune ni chūsha no hari o sasu isha no temoto ni 　atsumaru kokoro	the heart concentrated on the physician's hand putting the injection in the dead child's chest
soko shirenu nazo ni mukaite 　arugotoshi shiji no hitai ni matamo te o yaru	as though facing a fathomless riddle on the dead child's forehead again I place my hand
kanashimi no tsuyoku itaranu sabishisa yo waga ko no karada 　hiete yukedomo	how lonely to feel no grief though my child's body grows cold
kanashiku mo yo akuru made wa nokori-inu iki kireshi ko no hada no 　nukumori	pathetic the body of the child without breath warm till daybreak

There is no trace of sentimentality nor outburst of sorrow over the death of the shortlived baby. Takuboku simply describes the situation in as much detail as the thirty-one syllables permit. In fact, the simplicity of language and realism of description are what made it possible for him to put his personal grief under control, completely refined without a touch of pretense or exaggeration. This simplicity, however, the most eloquent expression of his sorrow as a father who has lost his first and only son, arouses all the more sympathy in the minds of those who read these lines. The boy's funeral was paid for by the money advanced by the publisher of *A Handful of Sand*.

II   Sad Toys

Sad Toys was published on June 20, 1912, about two months after Takuboku's death. The title of the book was chosen by Toki from the last words of "Various Things about Poetry," one of the two essays included in the volume. The collection contains 194 tanka, all written between the end of November, 1910, and August 21, 1911.

The tone of *Sad Toys* is reminiscent of that of the section "Love Songs to Myself" in *A Handful of Sand*, but with an added intensity and desperation, as evident in the two opening tanka of the collection:

ikisureba,
mune no uchi nite naru oto ari.
kogarashi yori mo
    sabishiki sono oto!

when I take a breath,
there's a rattle in my chest,
more desolate than
    a cold blast!

me tozuredo,
kokoro ni ukabu nani mo nashi.
sabishikumo, mata, me o
    akeru kana.

I close my eyes in meditation,
in my heart there is nothing.
from loneliness I
    open them again.

The intensity of feeling, whether of loneliness or despair, comes from the fact that Takuboku composed many of the tanka from his sickbed. His perception has become more realistic, centering on the details of his everyday life. Consequently, he no longer yearns much for the past, focusing instead on the time and place of his present life. Takuboku's final years were indeed ones of struggle, both physically and mentally.

Significantly, however, the intensity of feeling of *Sad Toys* is moderated by discipline of style. In order to heighten the effect of the words, Takuboku made two distinct stylistic innovations in these later tanka. First, for the use of simile, prominent in *A Handful of Sand*, Takuboku has substituted the use of various forms of punctuation. Takuboku had discovered that punctuation functions as effectively as simile in enlarging the poetic dimension of the tanka form. He uses punctuation, therefore, for a specific purpose and makes it an integral part of the tanka. Secondly, in *Sad Toys* Takuboku makes full use of the various possible arrangements of the thirty-one syllables of the tanka. While following most of the time the basic 5–7–5–7–7 syllabification Takuboku freely arranges it in three lines, ignoring the particular rhythm the division of the 5–7–5–7–7 syllabification usually creates. More than rhythm Takuboku places stress on the meaning of a tanka. Along with Takuboku's mastery of the three-line verse form, his flexibility in syllabification contributed to making his tanka close to free verse in the western style. Takuboku's conscious efforts, then, following the publication of *A Handful of Sand*, to bring about innovations in the tanka led to the discovery of a form and style most suited to his particular sensitivity and personality. This development, the result of strict discipline on his part, had the secondary effect of helping make the pain of his daily life more bearable.

One might say that in *Sad Toys* stylistic restraint is used as a protective shield against the encroachment of despair. In *Sad Toys*, therefore, more so than in *A Handful of Sand*, Takuboku comes forth as an accomplished artist of modern tanka, master of the style by which he could integrate form and content. Takuboku's originality lies in this development of his own unique style, which in turn gave new life to his treatment of the now old subject, the private world of his inner feelings.

Let us here examine some examples of Takuboku's new poetic development. Takuboku uses, for instance, exclamation marks to reveal the feelings of the characters presented in a situation:

tabi o omou otto no kokoro!	husband's heart thinking
shikari, naku, tsuma-ko no	of a trip!
kokoro!	scolding, crying, hearts of
asa no shokutaku!	wife and child!
	the breakfast table!

The function of exclamation points in this tanka is twofold. One is to make the reader visualize the situation at the breakfast table: the husband, longing for a moment of freedom, watching unconcernedly while his wife scolds their child; the other is to distinguish the kind and degree of sadness felt by the three individuals. That Takuboku can portray a scene of which he himself is a part with such detached objectivity is an indication of his maturation as a poet.

Two examples of the use of exclamation points for a different effect are:

kyō mo mata sake nomeru kana!	I drink sake again today!
sake nomeba	knowing I'll be upset
mune no mukatsuku kuse o	if I drink.
shiritsutsu.	

yamite areba kokoro mo   in sickness the heart, too,
    yowaruramu!   becomes weak!
samazama no   all kinds of sadness
nakitaki koto ga mune ni   collect in my chest.
    atsumaru.

The first tanka was written before Takuboku became ill and the
second after. In both cases various kinds of emotions felt by the poet
are conveyed by the exclamation points. In the last two lines following the punctuation mark the poet gives the reason for his pause,
and the exclamation point intensifies the sense of self-disgust implied in the last two lines. The punctuation in Takuboku's tanka calls
on the reader to exercise his own imagination, thereby bringing him
into the world of the poem, to feel what the poet feels and to grasp
intuitively the message hinted at by the punctuation. Other tanka in
which exclamation points are used for a similar effect are:

te mo ashi mo hanare-banare ni a fatigue like feet and hands
    aru gotoki   fallen off
monouki nezame!   melancholy awakening!
kanashiki nezame!   sad awakening!

jitto shite,   the wretched heart
mikan no tsuyu ni somaritaru   of one staring fixedly
    tsume o mitsumuru   at juice-stained
kokoro motonasa!   fingernails.

kamisama to giron shite   arguing with God and crying—
    nakishi—   that dream!
ano yume yo!   in the morning four days
yokka bakari mo mae no   ago.
    asa narishi.

me samashite sugu no   just wakened with a clear,
    kokoro yo!   pure heart!
toshiyori no iede no kiji nimo can't stop crying at the news
namida idetari.   of an old man who ran away
                                    from home.

Another mark of punctuation which Takuboku uses to fill a gap
between what is said and what is not said is the dash:

ie o dete gochō bakari wa,   leaving the house,
yō no aru hito no gotoku ni   like one on an errand,
aruite mitaredo—   walked about five blocks—

atarashiki asu no kitaru o
   shinzu to yū
jibun no kotoba ni
uso wa nakeredo—

when I say
I believe a new day is coming
I am not lying—

warau nimo waraware-zariki—
nagai koto sagashita naifu no
te no naka ni arishi ni.

no laughing matter—
the knife I searched for
   all that time
was in my hand.

In these tanka what is left unsaid, indicated by dashes, is what the poet wishes most to stress. The silence created by these dashes intensifies the sense of the frustration, anxiety and anger by which the sensitive poet is incessantly tormented.

The dash is also used for creating a different kind of effect:

omou koto nusumi-kikaruru
   gotoku nite,
tsuto mune o hikinu—
chōshinki yori.

as if my thoughts were
   being overheard,
suddenly pulled my chest
   back—
from the stethoscope.

unmei no kite noreru ka to
utagainu—
futon no omoki yowa no
   nezame ni.

wondered if my fate
had jumped up on my bed—
wakened up by the
   heavy quilt.

atarashiki sarado no iro no
ureshisa ni,
hashi toriagete mi wa
   mitsuredomo—

delighted with the fresh
   lettuce leaves
I pick up my chopsticks,
but I cannot eat—

mō uso o iwaji to omoiki—
sore wa kesa—
ima mata hitotsu uso o
   ieru kana.

I'll tell no more lies—
that was this morning—
now I've already told
   another one.

aru hi, futo, yamai o wasure,
ushi no naku mane o
   shiteminu,—
tsuma-ko no rusu ni.

one day, momentarily forgetting
   sickness,
I tried mooing like a cow,—
while my wife and child
   were out.

In each of the above examples, by using a dash Takuboku has created a dramatic situation with activity. The first tanka, for example, shows the poet pulling himself back from a doctor's stethoscope as if to protect his secret thoughts from being overheard. In the pause produced by the dash, the reader can feel the poet's fear, hope and curiosity, focused all at once on the stethoscope. Similarly, in the second tanka one can immediately visualize the poet in the middle of the night trying to move the quilted bed cover to ease his feeling of oppression. The dashes function as stage directions in a dramatic piece, enabling the reader to follow the movements of the poet's heart. A similar use of a dash can be seen in another tanka:

yogoretaru te o miru—	my dirty hands—
chōdo	looking at them is like
konogoro no jibun no kokoro ni	looking at my heart.
mukau ga gotoshi.	

In this poem, the best example of Takuboku's purposeful manipulation of the tanka syllabication, the dash spotlights the poet looking at his soiled hands, which he, Macbeth-like, sees as symbolic of the state of his heart.

Of all punctuation marks the most frequently used is the comma:

bon'yari to shita kanashimi ga,	a vague sadness,
yo to nareba,	when night falls,
nedai no ue ni sotto	comes and jumps upon my bed.
kite noru.	

The commas, which indicate a pause after one action before another follows, at the end of the first and the second lines enable the reader to understand sadness through the concrete visual image of a pet (presumably a cat) creeping silently into a room at night and jumping gently onto the bed. Thus through the use of commas along with the image of a tamed pet, Takuboku has created a serene tone, which shows that he has come to terms with sorrow, embracing it with calm resolution. Even sadness, which has been a constant tormentor of his life, has become a friendly visitor to a heart now accustomed to it.

To quote some other tanka well controlled by commas:

aonuri no seto no hibachi ni	leaning on the blue china
yorikakari,	hibachi,
me toji, me o ake,	closed my eyes, opened them
toki o oshimeri.	again,
	just to kill time.

suppori to futon o kaburi,
ashi o chijime,
shita no dashite minu, dare ni
  tomo nashini.

pull the quilt clear over
  my head,
pull up my legs,
stick out my tongue,
  at nobody.

ko o shikareba,
naite, neirinu.
kuchi sukoshi akeshi negao ni
  sawarite miru kana.

scolded, in tears the child
  fell asleep,
with her mouth half open.
I touched her sleeping face.

yamai iezu,
shinazu,
higoto ni kokoro nomi kewashiku
  nareru nana-yatsuki kana.

not getting well,
not dying,
a heart growing daily
  more bitter.

nanigoto ka ima ware
  tsubuyakeri.
kaku omoi,
me o uchitsuburi, ei o ajiwau.

muttered something just now.
so thinking,
closed my eyes, to enjoy
  being drunk.

arano yuku kisha no gotoku ni,
kono nayami,
tokidoki ware no kokoro o tōru.

like a train through
  a wasteland,
this suffering at times,
runs across my heart.

yamite shigatsu—
sono ma nimo, nao, meni miete,
waga ko no setake nobishi
  kanashimi.

four months since I fell ill—
during that time, I can see
my daughter's grown
  that much.

The period is another punctuation mark with which Takuboku achieves unity between the form and the content of a tanka. Let us look at the following:

tonomo niwa hanetsuku
  oto su.
warau koe su.
kyonen no shōgatsu ni kaereru
  gotoshi.

outdoors the sound of
  the shuttlecock.
laughing voices.
like returning to last
  year's New Year.

nan to naku,
kotoshi wa yoi koto
  arugotoshi.
ganjitsu no asa, harete
  kaze nashi.

there's the feeling somehow,
this will be a good year.
the New Year morning,
  bright and calm.

In the first example by using a period at the end of each line Takuboku shows himself becoming aware of the sounds from out of

doors as he lies indoors confined to his bed. They are the typical
sounds of New Year's Day, sounds of the shuttlecock and of laughter. He lets them sink into his consciousness one by one, his moments of reflection indicated by the periods. The last line brings the
two sounds together and combines them with the poet's recollections of New Year's Days of the past, when he, too, was participating
in the games and the laughter. In the second piece, the period at the
end of the second line emphasizes the poet's sentiment: he is convinced (or perhaps wants very much to be convinced) that something good will happen this year. In the last line he describes the
beautiful clear day with no wind, surely a harbinger of good fortune,
which has brought him to this conclusion.

A period by separating two parts of a tanka may also serve to
heighten a sense of alienation:

hito ga mina	everybody's
onaji hōgaku ni muite yuku.	going in the same direction.
sore o yoko yori	the heart of one who
mite iru kokoro.	watches from the side.

The periods used in this tanka point up the emotional distance
between the poet and others by creating a sensation of steady
movement in the first sentence and a feeling of marking time in the
second. The sense of movement is produced by the uninterrupted
flow of the first two lines: the people are all going in the same
direction unimpeded by someone moving in an opposite direction
just as the lines describing them are unimpeded by punctuation.
The sentence ends with a verb ("*yuku*"—"go"), making the reader's
last impression of the people one of movement. The period effectively separates this active society from the solitary world of the poet
who stands on the sidelines, watching these people going their own
way. The noun ending of the last line ("*kokoro*"—"heart") emphasizes the static feeling.

Finally let us look at an example in which Takuboku uses a
comma, a period and a question mark:

kono shigonen,	these four or five years,
sora o aogu to yū koto ga	I haven't once looked up
ichido mo nakariki.	at the sky.
kō mo narumono ka?	could this really have
	happened?

The comma carries the feeling of a downward look and forces a pause as if a person is moving slowly, thoughtfully. The period brings the poem to a complete stop: the poet is stunned to realize how preoccupied he has been. In the last line a question has already been indicated by the particle *"ka"*; the addition of a question mark stresses the poet's incredulity that he has developed such a pattern of life.

Takuboku conducts one further experiment with method. He gives a direct quotation of a statement made to him and his own reaction to it:

"Ishikawa wa fubin na yatsu da."
toki ni kō jibun de iite,
kanashimite miru.

"Ishikawa is a pitiful fellow."
sometimes saying this to
    myself,
I make myself sad.

sonnaraba inochi ga hoshiku-
    nai no ka to,
isha ni iwarete,
damarishi kokoro!

then you really don't want
    to live?
scolded by my physician,
my heart gave no answer!

mō omae no shintei o yoku
    mitodoketa to,
yume ni haha kite
naite yukishi kana.

I know what you're thinking.
in a dream my mother appeared
and weeping went away.

jitto shite nete irasshai to
kodomo ni demo yū ga gotoku ni
isha no yū hi kana.

now just be quiet and rest.
as though talking to a child
the day the physician said that.

In the first tanka the speaker is the poet's own superego; the other tanka quote his mother or his physician. In every instance, however, the poet is faced with an authority figure, someone passing judgment on him or in some other way treating him as a child. It is this pointing up of his imagined shortcomings which evokes his own internal reaction. This miniature dialogue makes the tanka as dramatic as the short form will allow. The use of direct quotations creates living people in an actual situation, thus bringing a new realism to the tanka form, a legacy perhaps of Takuboku's early apprenticeship in novel writing.

As was observed at the beginning of this section, many of Takuboku's last tanka, written from a sickbed, were more than ever concerned with the details of his present life, fast slipping away from him. Of all of his everyday worries Takuboku's parents were always among his chief concerns; they appear again in the tanka of *Sad Toys*.

Takuboku's father had become a drifter like his son after he failed to regain his position at Hōtoku Temple at Shibutami. When Takuboku moved in August into a house after leaving the hospital in the spring of 1911, Ittei joined his son's household:

kanashiki wa waga chichi!
kyō mo shimbun o yomi akite,
niwa ni koari to asoberi.

my pitiful father!
today again bored with
    reading the newspaper,
he plays with the ants
    in the garden.

The son's verse vividly catches the tragedy of the father's life. A man in the prime of life, formerly a person held in high respect in his community, deprived of position, esteem and livelihood, is now passing his days to no purpose dependent on an invalid son.

Takuboku's mother seems torn between determined hope and frustration:

cha made tachite,
waga heifu¹ ɔ inoritamau
haha no kyō mata nanika
    ikareru.

even giving up her
    favorite tea,
to pray for my recovery
what is Mother angry about
    today?

Giving up the tea she is so fond of is for her a form of abstinence or fasting as she prays for her son's recovery. Her faith and patience, however, are wearing thin as her prayers seem to fall on deaf ears. The disruption of her own household, long separations from her husband, the illness of her son and lack of compatibility with her daughter-in-law, aggravated by poverty and privation and her own poor health, all contribute to her frequent outbursts of temper.

Takuboku, now a parent himself, can empathize with his parents' expectations of him. He realizes that as the only son he was the recipient of special favors and the focus of special hopes. Even their present misfortune is of course due to their overindulgence of their son. Takuboku, now confined to bed, can only feel remorse at his inability to help them, a feeling mingled, no doubt, with guilt over the singleminded pursuit of his own ideals:

tada hitori no
otoko no ko naru ware wa
　　kaku sodateri.
fubo mo kanashikaruramu.

to have their only son
turn out like this.
my parents must surely be
　　grieving.

From the standpoint of subject matter one particular area of concentration in *Sad Toys* is the world of a sick person. Some of the pieces have already been cited; here we see others which catch feelings of hopelessness, loneliness and the suppressed yet ever present fear of death, written while Takuboku was in the hospital:

fukuretaru hara o nadetsutsu,
byōin no nedai ni, hitori,
kanashimite ari.

stroking my swollen stomach,
in the hospital bed, alone,
in sorrow.

doa oshite hitoashi dereba,
byōnin no me ni hatemonaki
nagarōka kana.

push the door open and step
　　out,
to the eyes of the sick person
the long corridor seems endless.

mayonaka ni futo me ga samete,
wake mo naku nakitaku narite,
futon o kabureru.

awaking in the middle of
　　the night,
for no reason wanting to cry,
pull the quilt over my head.

hanashi kakete
　　henji no naki ni
yoku mireba,
naite itariki, tonari no kanja.

no reply
then I notice he is crying,
the patient in the next bed.

yoru osoku doko yara no
　　heya no sawagashiki wa
hito ya shinitaramu to,
iki o hisomuru.

late at night, from somewhere
　　a stir
has someone died, maybe?
I hold my breath.

In the monotonous daily routine details take on an added significance:

myaku o toru kangofu no te no,
atatakaki hi ari,
tsumetaku kataki hi mo ari.

the hand of the nurse
　　checking pulses,
some days warm,
some days hard and cold.

myaku o toru te no furui koso
kanashikere—
isha ni shikarare
　　wakaki kangofu!

the trembling of the hand
　　that checks my pulse
has a special sadness—
the young nurse scolded by
　　the physician!

Yet the stay in the hospital has had some good effects as well on Takuboku's feelings. The separation from his family and respite from the cares of their daily life has called forth more positive feelings for them:

byōin ni kite,   in the hospital,
tsuma ya ko o itsukushimu   love my wife and child
makoto no ware ni   I've found myself again.
    kaerikeru kana.

As we have seen in both *A Handful of Sand* and *Sad Toys* Takuboku made of his tanka a poetic journal of his private life, recorded in thirty-one syllable entries. This personalization of the tanka was a marked break with tradition, the significance of which cannot be overemphasized. From the time of the *Man'yōshū*, which was compiled in the middle of the eighth century, the traditional subject matter of tanka had been the world of nature. Furthermore, Takuboku's break with traditional subject matter led also to a break with traditional form. Tanka convention called for the poet to produce a regular phrasal sequence in a syllabic count of 5-7-5-7-7 while achieving a perfect unity between the sound of the words and the image they create. It was generally felt that writing the thirty-one syllables in one single line was the most effective way to accomplish this. In his employment of the three-line form, Takuboku liberated himself from the restraints of the long tanka tradition and opened the way for further modifications. As Odagiri Hideo points out:

Rather than the traditional unity in meter and rhythm, Takuboku has moved toward a form and style that correspond to the content, the meaning of a tanka. While preserving the basic form of the tanka, and while maintaining the method of creating the intended unified effect by combining imagery and the sound of words . . . , by organizing a tanka in three lines he tried to develop a new possibility in the tanka. Takuboku did not abandon the basic traditional frame of the tanka in which the poet condenses the reality of humanity into thirty-one syllables . . . ; he merely expanded its originality, and made of the tanka a poetic expression most appropriate for the description of truthful experience of humanity. By using three lines for the tanka, Takuboku has brought the tanka closer to poetry, which has flexibility in form according to its content.[5]

The world of Takuboku's tanka is that of his actual life brought into sharp focus. It is the private world of one individual, but the personal feelings of that individual transformed into art of lasting value. In this sense, one can say that it is the most personal tanka that possess universal quality. Takuboku drew his tanka from the deepest levels of his emotional experience, the most human experience of all.

CHAPTER 6

The Takuboku Legacy

O F all the literary figures Meiji Japan produced, few writers, with the possible exception of Natsume Sōseki, have among the general public enjoyed such lasting popularity as Takuboku. The inner strength with which he confronted a life of privation, the determined will to keep his youthful creative energy active in the face of poverty, and the independent spirit with which he fearlessly spoke up for the value of individualism have won for him the admiration of his readers and have made him an almost legendary figure. Idolized by old and young, rich and poor, Takuboku continues to live as the symbol of eternal youth in the minds and hearts of those who enjoy literature.

Takuboku's popularity, however, is due almost entirely to his tanka, in which his influence on subsequent generations is most apparent. In neither poetry nor the novel did Takuboku produce anything of sufficient substance to establish a literary reputation. His contribution to the history of modern poetry is significant for his introduction of new subjects for poetry, especially socialism. In this respect the influence of *Power and Poetry* on the proletarian writers of the 1920s is considerable. Yet the image of Takuboku preserved by these writers is not so much that of an artist as that of a thinker. It is the ideas sung forth in *Power and Poetry* they took seriously.

As a novelist Takuboku failed to produce a work equal in quality to his tanka. His novels are read simply because they are his, not because of any particular intrinsic literary merit. Takuboku's novels did not pioneer new possibilities for the genre to the extent that his tanka did. Even his comparatively successful works such as *The Hospital Window*, *The Shadow of a Bird* and *Our Gang and He* are valuable only in the sense that they point to Takuboku's potential. In these novels he deals with ideas which are certainly ahead of their time, but his artistic accomplishment does not match that of such

172

novelists as Ōgai, Tōson and Sōseki. The great irony of Takuboku's career is that he achieved lasting fame not through the novel, the form which he regarded most highly, but through the tanka, which he considered no more than a toy.

I *Takuboku the Essayist*

Even though Takuboku's poetry and novels can be disregarded in the evaluation of his position in modern Japanese literature, his essays must not be ignored. As Takuboku the artist is most clearly revealed in his tanka, so in his essays is Takuboku the critic is most eloquently manifested.

Takuboku's essays reveal a remarkable sensitivity to the spirit of the age. Whether the issue was education, literature or politics, he intuitively saw through to the core of the problem and pointed it out fearlessly. Though often driven by impulse, he remained faithful to the dictates of conscience. His critical mind was kept active by a passion for new ideas for bringing forth a new world better than the present existing one. It is this zeal for the new, combined with a discriminating sensibility, that led him to develop his advanced views of life and literature and that enabled him to produce such a penetrating essay as "The Present State of the Age of Repression." It is only natural that Takuboku's farsighted view and unyielding voice calling attention to the injustices of an autocratic society should lead to his being posthumously placed in a position of mentor to the proletarian writers in the 1920s. The publication of "The Present State of the Age of Repression" gave them the courage to speak up for the weak and the oppressed. Concerning the literary impact of this essay upon the succeeding decade, Watanabe Junzō, one of the proletarian writers, has this to say:

At the end of the essay Takuboku says that "criticism is what my literature seeks." A few years after Takuboku's death, namely around 1916 or 1917, a literary movement called proletarian literature came into existence for the first time in Japan. It was a literature produced from the viewpoint of the working class, which was to carry the future of Japan on their shoulders. . . . It was a literature born out of the desire "to discover the necessity of tomorrow for our own sake." Further, it was naturally a kind of literature that declared war against "the present state of the age of repression." For the development of society and for the history of literature the rise of this type of literary movement was indispensable. In this sense, Takuboku's "The Present State of the Age of Repression" has given direction to the

development of modern Japanese literature and proved itself to be the
predecessor of the proletarian literary movement.[1]

This essay along with "From Yumi-chō: Poems to Eat," an essay in a
similar vein, sharpened for the proletarian writers the image of
Takuboku as a writer for the common man. Takuboku thus came to
be regarded as a person of profound sympathy for the poor as well as
a strong exponent of freedom of the individual as the right of anyone
regardless of social status. This passionate democratic sentiment
places him among the most eloquent and foresighted critics Japan
has produced in the last hundred years.

II   *Takuboku the Tanka Poet*

Along with Toki Aika, Takuboku is today considered a co-founder
of the tanka group called *seikatsu-ha,* whose objective it was to sing
about daily life. The group began to be so called after the publication of a magazine by Toki in 1913, *Life and the Arts,* a magazine
intended to be in the vein of Takuboku's abortive magazine,
Tree and Fruit. Its editorial policy was to attempt a narrowing
of the gap between literature and life; Takuboku's tanka
being an exemplar of what the magazine endorsed, he was
regarded as the champion of the group. As a result tanka of similar
style and subject matter to those of Takuboku and Toki since that
time have been known as tanka of *seikatsu-ha.* The group stressed
the importance of writing the tanka in three lines, and made it
their motto to deal directly with the actualities of everyday existence, particularly with its hardships. Furthermore, in order to describe candidly such mundane details, they considered it imperative
to bring poetic expression closer to the language of everyday conversation to generate a more immediate empathic bond between the
reader and the situation presented in the tanka. Their style is thus
individualistic and reflects a genuine attempt at reaching a wider
reading public through the medium of the tanka.

A.   *Takuboku and Toki Aika*

The relationship of Toki and Takuboku lasted no more than a year
because of the latter's untimely death, but the influence which these
two young tanka poets had on each other was considerable. The
device of writing the tanka in three lines, first introduced by Toki in
Tears and Laughter, was a great stimulus to Takuboku. It is appar-

ent that Toki also was much encouraged by the appearance of another tanka poet, more gifted than himself, who could appreciate the three-line method and could grasp and expand its potential.

After Takuboku's death Toki published tanka that reveal an obvious similarity to Takuboku's both in content and style. Take the following for example:

te no shiroki rōdōsha koso
  kanashikere.
kokkin no sho o
namida shite yomeri.

sad indeed the laborer
  with white hands.
he reads a banned book
with tears in his eyes.

waga tomo no, shindai no
  shita no
kaban yori
kokkin no sho o karite
  yuku kana.

from the suitcase
under my friend's bed
I borrowed the banned book.

dokutoru no chōshinki o kari,
waga mune ni ategaeba,—ya,
oto ga suru, oto ga suru.

borrowing the doctor's
  stethoscope,
I placed it on my chest—hear!
beating! beating!

tsuto gakeyori sakashimani
  otsuru
kono yume o,
konogoro matamo shikirini
  miru kana.

suddenly I plunge headlong
from a cliff—I've often
  been
having this dream lately.

These can be compared with four of Takuboku's:

te ga shiroku
katsu dai nariki
hibon naru hito to iwaruru
  otoko ni aishi ni

his hands were white
but very large
he was no ordinary man

akagami no hyōshi tezureshi
kokkin no
fumi o kōri no soko ni
  sagasu hi

the banned book with the
  worn red cover
the day I searched for it
in the bottom of the trunk

omou koto nusumi-kikaruru
  gotoku nite,
tsuto mune o hikinu—
chōshinki yori.

as if my thoughts were
  being overheard,
suddenly pulled my chest
  back—
from the stethoscope.

nani ga nashi ni	somewhere in my head
atama no naka ni gake arite	there's a kind of cliff
higoto ni tsuchi no	crumbling away
kuzururu gotoshi	

While revealing a deep affinity with Takuboku, Toki neverthe-less maintained his own individuality. Besides being the first person to write tanka in three lines, he was also the first to use punctuation in tanka; and so even before meeting Takuboku, Toki had already made a name for himself as an innovative tanka poet. The following example, ("ko to, tsuma to, gejo to,/ omocha to,/ ware to,—mina,/ hone ga barabara ni naritaru/ gotoshi") *"my child, wife, maid, toys,/ and I,—all are like/scattered bones"* shows his skillful use of punctua-tion to enhance the meaning of the words. Other representative tanka by Toki include the following:

hataraku tame ni ikeru ni ya aramu,	am I living to work,
ikuru tame ni hatarakeru ni ya,	or working to live?
wakaranaku nareri.	I don't know which.

kuruhoshiku, tsuyoki tabako o	pulling on a strong cigarette
suishi ato,	like mad,
tōku, Shiberia no	I think of the snow
yuki o omoeri.	in far away Siberia.

ware nariki,—kano toshi no	it was I—a young man
natsu,	the summer of that year
furari to yuki, furari to	sauntered in, sauntered out.
sarishi	
ichi seinen wa.	

atsumarite, warera no katarishi	in the room next to ours
isshitsu no,	where we gathered to talk,
fusuma no soto no	my mother's coughing.
haha no seki kana.	

hijō naru akuji wa naki ka.	isn't there any extraordinary
zensekai no,	evil?
oto to yū oto no shinihatsuru	such an evil that would silence
hodo no,—	all the noises of the world.

futo,—shin'ya no machi o	wandering around town
tadorite,	late at night,
kanashiminu,	I was sad,
aware, hisashiku umi o	what a pity—I've not seen
mizaru kana.	the sea for so long.

Although Toki's craftsmanship compares favorably with that of Takuboku, his tanka as a whole lack the depth of feeling and emotional intensity of Takuboku's. Further, Toki's tanka show a want of poetic subtlety: they tend to become no more than mere statements in spite of the poet's careful manipulation of structure and punctuation.

The difference between Toki's and Takuboku's tanka is partly due to differences in the personal circumstances of the two poets. Toki was a college graduate; his social position was guaranteed and he did not suffer from poverty as Takuboku did. In short, Toki's life was removed from the kind of despair and intense passions Takuboku experienced and which gave birth to tanka of rich feeling and abundant variety. The difference is also due to a difference in personality, which can be detected in the distinct tones of their respective tanka. Toki's tanka are more detached than personal, more intellectual than emotional and more restrained and gentle than impulsive.

B. *Takuboku and the Proletarian Poets*

In 1923 Yasunari Jirō (1888–1974) published an article in *Chūōkōron* entitled "Takuboku as a Proletarian Poet and Others," which gives us a general idea of how Takuboku was received among tanka circles in the years immediately following his death. Yasunari explains the reason for his decision to write the essay:

According to the topic designated for this article two points are taken for granted: one is that there exists a group of poets called proletarian poets and that there are arts belonging to a specific social class; the other is that Takuboku's art belongs to a certain social class. These two points are already accepted by many, and when I was asked by the editor to write an article on the subject I did not even give it second thought. But after a reexamination of Takuboku's tanka, I became interested in evaluating the validity of the general consensus of Takuboku as a proletarian poet.

As is clear from this statement, Takuboku had been regarded as a pioneer of proletarian literature, which became the central literary movement of the 1920s. While Yasunari holds some reservation about labeling Takuboku as a proletarian poet, he at the same time stresses the importance of the proletarian sentiment of many of Takuboku's tanka, as, for example, evident in the following group:

hyākushō no ōku wa sake o
    yameshi to yū.
motto komaraba,
nani o yameruramu.
	I hear many farmers
	    have quit drinking.
	when their life becomes
	    even harder,
	what will they give up?

tomo mo tsuma mo kanashi to
    omou rashi—
yamai mite mo nao,
kakumei no koto kuchi ni
    tataneba.
	friends and wife seem
	    to think it pitiful
	for me to keep talking
	    about revolution
	even in sickbed.

hirate mote
fubuki ni nureshi kao o fuku
tomo kyōsan o shugi to
    serikeri
	wet by a snowstorm
	my friend wipes his face
	    with his palm
	he's now a confirmed communist

urukoto o sashitomerareshi hon no chosha ni michi nite aeru aki no asa kana	the autumn morning I met on the street the author of the book whose sale had been banned
hatarakedo hatarakedo nao kurashi raku ni narazaru jitto te o miru	I work and work but my life still gets no better I stare at my hands

Because the proletarian poets believed the proper role of literature was to awaken the reader to correct the injustices of society, it was only natural that Takuboku's tanka dealing with the hardships of his own life became the center of their literary interest. These poets tended therefore to pay less attention to those of Takuboku's tanka that deal with his private inner world. For the proletarian poets the scope of the *seikatsu-ha* tanka as established by Takuboku was too limited to represent the voice of "the masses." They concentrated therefore on extending the perspective of the *seikatsu-ha* group by making their own tanka more society oriented. Let us here examine in three tanka poets, Yasunari Jirō, Nishimura Yōkichi and Watanabe Junzō, how Takuboku's tanka evolved after his death.

C. *Takuboku and Yasunari Jirō*

The author of the article referred to above was a tanka poet who himself holds a kind of transitional position between the *seikatsu-ha* and the proletarian group. Although he does not consider himself a proletarian poet, Yasunari admits that some of the tanka he wrote, particularly in his youth, reflect proletarian sentiments. For instance, in his first published collection of tanka, *Poverty and Love* (1916), he included the following: ("toyo ashihara mizuho no kuni ni/ umarekite/ kome ga kuenu to wa/ uso no yo na hanashi") "born in Japan/ and unable to ear rice—unbelievable" Yasunari himself was fond of this piece, and it indeed astutely presents the irony of a situation brought on by poverty. Other tanka with proletarian overtones are:

kane koso wa kanashikere—
ōshū no taisen mo,
ware to tsuma to no monchaku mo
   kono tame.

money is the root of
   all evil—
wars in Europe
and quarrels with my wife,
   all begin there.

kōjinbutsu to,
ware o iishi otoko ni kane o
   karite,
kaesazu, konogoro wa nan to
   yūran.

I borrowed money
from a man who once called me
   a good guy.
I've not returned it—what
   does he call me now?

kane no aru otoko no tsura ga
kinikuwazu
hige ni hi o tsukete
   moyashite yarōka.

I get disgusted
at a wealthy man's face
shall I set his moustache
   on fire?

binbō na ie kara erai
   mono ga deru
sore o tanoshimi ni
kodomo o kosaeru.

"a great man comes from a
   poor home"
believing in this saying
I beget children.

yoru osoku kaereba,
tsuma no nete itari,
sono kao o mite yo ga
   iya ni naru.

came home late
wife already asleep
seeing her face grew sick
   of the world.

The first and the second examples echo Takuboku's tanka:

waga daku shisō wa subete
kane naki ni insuru gotoshi
aki no kaze fuku

all my philosophies
seem to stem from poverty
the autumn wind blows

jitsumu ni wa yaku ni tatazaru
   utabito to
ware o miru hito ni
kane karinikeri

from a man who thinks of me
as unpractical
I borrowed money

After the publication of *Poverty and Love* Yasunari continued to
write tanka, some of which he has quoted in the above mentioned
essay:

kū tame ni
isshōkenmei hataraite,
namida o nagasu, mazushii
    shokuzen ni.

after working so hard
just to eat,
I weep over the poor food
    on the table.

ato ni umareru mono no tame ni,
nanika hitotsu no koto o
    nasan,
genzai no seikatsu ni
    tsukareru mae ni.

for those to be born
    after me,
I wish to do something,
before I am worn out with
    this present life.

inu ni soete,
inu ni kuwaseyo to
    kureshi pan o
inu ni kuwasezu, kora ga
    kuinikeri.

a piece of bread
given for our dog—
my children have eaten it.

anma o sasete,
karada ga raku ni narinikeri,
kurashi muki no anma wa
    aranu ka.

after getting a massage
my body feels good all over
no way to get a massage
    for everyday life?

Although the scope of these tanka does not go beyond that of the
seikatsu-ha, Yasunari has succeeded in conveying private feelings
about his daily life. The feelings expressed, spontaneous and
genuine, are set forth in a simple style free from pretense or exaggeration. To sing about the poet's private life with objectivity and
sincerity is exactly what Takuboku practiced in his tanka. In Yasunari's tanka one can see that the spirit of Takuboku's tanka is preserved along with his clarity of expression.

D.   *Takuboku and Nishimura Yōkichi*

Nishimura Yōkichi (1892–1959)—poet, editor and publisher—
holds a unique place in the history of modern tanka. He was respon-
sible for the publication of Takuboku's *A Handful of Sand* and *Sad
Toys* and Toki's *Life and the Arts*. He edited and published his own
literary magazines, *The Blue Table* (1914) and *A Small Land* (1920),
for which he collected tanka by socialist and proletarian poets.
Further, Nishimura was a minor tanka poet himself, first as an active

seikatsu-ha and later as a proletarian poet. He published two collections of his own tanka under the titles of *City Dwellers* and *Trees Along a Street*. To quote some of his works:

shigoto no hima,
sangai ni noboreba Tokyo no,
sora hirobiro to aki no
    kaze fukeri.

between working hours,
I go up to the third floor.
in the vast sky of Tokyo
the autumn breeze.

shigonin no jokō ga sumi ni
    katamarite,
bentō kuinu,
hiru no kōjō.

four or five girls sit
    together in a corner,
eating their lunch,
in a factory at noon.

Kitakami no kawamizu midashi,
shigonin ga uma arai ori,
Takuboku wa nashi.

stirring Kitakami's stream,
men washing horses,
Takuboku's gone.

don'yori to kumorite samuki
nippon no
mazushiki fuyu to nari ni
    keru kana

heavily overcast and cold
Japan's winter of privation
has come

nippon no seinen ware wa
isu ni mamashi tabako o suite
Roshia o omou

a young man of Japan
sitting idly in a chair
    and smoking
thinking of Russia

Inspired by Takuboku's "After Endless Discussions," Nishimura also wrote the following:

ichiza mina
fuhei to narishi seinen no,
kono kokoro o ba
    izuchi e yaran.

the youth here
are all frustrated
what fills their hearts?

warera mina,
kotogotoku genjō ni yasunzezu,
kakute itsumade tsuzukan to
    suru ka.

every one of us
is discontent with the present,
how much longer will it last?

Written in simple language, Nishimura's tanka are easy to understand. Yet most of his works lack deep feeling. Being a publisher, Nishimura was comparatively well-to-do and unable to empathize with the poor at the deepest level. That he himself was fully aware of this dilemma can be seen in his tanka:

kanemochi ni arazu,
saredo kūni mo owarezaru,
kono namanuruki seikatsu ni aku.

not rich,
but have enough to eat,
tired of this lukewarm life.

suhadaka no otoko to nashite
    kono ware ni,
suki o motasete
tsuchi o utashime.

strip me of all I have,
put a hoe in my hand
and make me till the soil.

ie mo kane mo aru kanashisa,
gogo no machi o burabura to,
ukanu kokoro ni aruki
    keru kana.

the sadness of having a house
    and money,
I walk the streets aimlessly,
on a gloomy afternoon.

More than through his tanka or his work as editor and publisher, however, Nishimura's most significant contribution was his theory of tanka, a theory that became in fact the manifesto of the *seikatsuha* and proletarian groups. He maintained that the tanka should be an art form of and for the common people, and therefore its aristocratic elitism should be abandoned. In order to realize this purpose, Nishimura believed, one should derive material for the tanka from the everyday world of work and struggle, not from the elegant world of a leisured class, heretofore regarded as the only appropriate source for tanka subjects. Nishimura's desire, in short, was to democratize the tanka and, though his tanka do not reach a high artistic level, as a proletarian poet he put his theory into practice.

E. *Takuboku and Watanabe Junzō*

Of the proletarian tanka poets influenced by Takuboku, Watanabe Junzō (1894–1972) surpassed the others in his achievement as a poet. Like Takuboku he lived a life of poverty, which naturally nourished his bent toward socialism. In his youth Watanabe was absorbed in Takuboku's tanka and has himself acknowledged his indebtedness to Takuboku, particularly to his socialistic thought. After the Russian Revolution in 1917, Watanabe became totally devoted to the cause of socialism. He had begun writing tanka at the age of fifteen or so, and as his interest in socialism increased his tanka as a means of showing deep empathy with working people as particularly the hardships of the poor. It was his intention to utilize tanka as a means of showing deep empathy with working people as he openly admitted: "Always I am with the people. I wish to sing about their sorrow, joy and anger as if they were my own and wish for the songs of my sorrow, joy and anger to echo theirs."[2] Watanabe's tanka are written in one line, the transition of ideas being indicated by spacing and punctuation. A few tanka from his *Songs of Privation* (1924) are quoted here. For convenience's sake they are quoted in three lines:

aware kono, misuborashisa o ika ni sen, kata ikarashite aruite miredo.	though I walk as if wealthy, nothing can be done about this poverty.
kuruma hiku, ware no sugata ga garasudo ni, utsurite miyuru samuki asa kana.	in the glass door, I see myself pulling a wagon— cold early morning.
hatarakedo—, hatarakedo itsumo mazushiku, makotoni haha mo yashinaenu ko wa.	I work and work— but always a poor son, unable to feed his mother.
waga shisō, ōkata wa yo ni irerarezu, runin no gotoku, kyō mo sabishimu.	in all probability, the world'll reject my thoughts, lonely again like an exile.
nanimo kamo haradatashikute, kyō ichinichi, mono mo iwaneba, kemono no gotoshi.	raging at everything, all day long silent. felt like a beast.

It is apparent that Watanabe obtained a number of ideas and images from Takuboku's tanka, but the feelings he conveys are his own. The well disciplined style shows no traces of the shallowness and superficiality seen in Nishimura's tanka.

As we have seen, the spirit of Takuboku's tanka, that is to say, the simplicity of style and language and subject matter taken from everyday life, was continued by the proletarian poets who thought of themselves as his successors. With the exception of Watanabe, however, whose tanka display forcefulness and genuine feeling, the proletarian poets on the whole tended to overlook the importance of maintaining high literary quality. They were primarily concerned with using the tanka as a means to voice their social protest but only secondarily concerned with it as an art form. It is ludicrous indeed that such pieces as the ones quoted below were regarded as poetry:

shimijimi to	a policeman who spoke
kono Asakusa de daraku suru	feelingly
hito no hanashi o	of men who go to ruin
kikaseta junsa	here in Asakusa
futokoro no	the tanka collection of Takuboku
Takuboku kashū—sono hon de	in my pocket—with that book
ore o nagutta Asakusa no junsa	the Asakusa policeman hit me
asekusai zubon o nugeba	when I take off the sweaty
poketto ni zeni no	trousers
oto ga suru	coins jingle in the pocket
tsukareta tsukareta	tired, tired

In these examples there is no trace of the artistic subtlety or restraint that makes the tanka what it is. These resemble the tanka
only in their employment of thirty-one syllables.

What is apparent is that Takuboku's tanka because of its seeming
artless simplicity was too often treated superficially and abused. The
fact that Takuboku's successors, however, failed to measure up to
his own high standards does not mean that his tanka is at fault. It is
in fact in this very comparison of Takuboku with those who attempted to imitate him that one can see the greatness of his achievement.
The unity of feeling and style which makes Takuboku's tanka outstanding is born from his personal inner life. It is the result of an
artistic discipline governing these strong emotions, a discipline
which the majority of Takuboku's followers did not have. Following
Takuboku's style alone therefore does not bring forth the kind of
tanka Takuboku himself composed. Herein lies indeed the uniqueness of his work.

There is some justification, as Yasunari pointed out, for the proletarian poets' regarding Takuboku as the forerunner of their kind of
literature, because he did write some tanka of proletarian sentiment. Tanka that may be regarded as distinctly socialistic, however,
make up only a small portion of the works Takuboku produced.
Writing about a particular social class— or the members of that
class—was not Takuboku's primary concern. What he wrote about
was his own life; he wrote about others only as he came into contact
with them, only as their lives touched his own. Takuboku was led
primarily by an instinct to probe into the reality of human experience as well as his innate compassion for his fellow human beings.
Such motivating forces transcend any political ideology or economic

system. The tanka, for Takuboku a mirror reflecting everything he was familiar with in both his external and internal worlds, as such, constituted an artistic means for him to attain self-knowledge. By singing of *his* problems, *his* feelings, the private voice in his tanka became the voice of all people.

F. *Takuboku and Saitō Mokichi*

Takuboku's influence is not confined to those ideological poets who regarded him as the predecessor of their school. His place in the history of modern tanka must also be evaluated in relation to such a representative modern tanka poet as Saitō Mokichi (1882–1953). Saitō, an innovator of the tanka in his own right, was the central figure of the *"Araragi* School" which emphasized realistic portrayal of life in the composition of tanka. About Saitō's works Akutagawa Ryūnosuke remarked in his essay, "Literary, Too Literary" (1927): "In *Red Light* Saitō Mokichi composed a series of tanka under the titles of 'Mother Who Has Passed Away' and 'Ohiro'. Not only that. He has been steadily completing what Ishikawa Takuboku left off about fifteen years ago—what is called the *'seikatsu-ha'* tanka."[3] The volume Akutagawa refers to, *Red Light*, was Saitō's first collection of tanka, published in 1913, one year after Takuboku's death. Although Saitō makes no mention of Takuboku's influence, as Akutagawa points out, Saitō's perception as revealed in "Mother Who Has Passed Away" clearly shows a Takuboku-like sensitivity. Some tanka from the series are cited below. As with Watanabe's tanka Saitō's originals written in one line are put in three lines here:

michinoku no haha no inochi o
hitome min hitome mintozo
tada ni isogeru

while Mother's still alive
I hurry home
for one last look one look

shi ni chikaki haha ni soine no
shinshin to tōda no kawazu
ten ni kikoyuru

beside my dying mother,
all calm
the frogs' cries in the far
field reach heaven

shi ni chikaki hahaga me ni yori
odamaki no hana sakitari to
ii ni keru kana

bending over the eyes of
my dying mother
I say to her: "A columbine
flower
has bloomed."

inochi aru hito atsumarite | living people gathered around
waga haha no inochi shiyuku o | watched it leave,
mitari shiyuku o | my mother's life leave

waga haha o | I stand with a torch
yakaneba naranu hi o moteri | to cremate Mother
amatsu-sora ni wa | nothing to look at in the sky
   miru mono mo nashi |

hoshi no iru | under the star-lit sky
yozora no moto ni aka-aka to | a body, Mother's body,
hahasowa no haha wa | burns in red flames
   moeyuki ni keri |

hai no naka ni haha o hiroeri | I pick out Mother in the
asahiko no noboru ga naka ni | ashes
haha o hiroeri | in the morning sun as it rises
  | I pick out Mother

sabishisa ni taete wakeiru | in loneliness
yamakage ni kuroguro to | I go into a mountain cove
akebi no hana chiri ni keri | the akebia flowers lie
  | scattered black

These poems remind us of the tanka Takuboku wrote in memory of his son. The potentially sentimental subject is put under masterful control through detached realism. Saitō's language is more stylized than Takuboku's and in his concrete objective description he has succeeded in crystallizing the overpowering feeling of sorrow manifested in each line. The sincerity with which Saitō portrays his intense personal feeling is indeed identical with Takuboku's.

Whether or not Saitō recognized it, the fact that his tanka reveal the Takuboku-like concreteness and intensity in his treatment of events of his daily life shows the characteristic pattern of Takuboku's influence on other poets. It is no exaggeration to say that not only Takuboku's contemporaries but succeeding generations of tanka poets whether they are aware of it or not write in the shadow of Takuboku. Takuboku's innovations changed the very nature of the tanka both in style and content. Today tens of thousands of people write tanka, and while maintaining the basic tanka form exhibit a greater flexibility in handling a variety of subjects. Many modern tanka deal with the concrete personal world of the poet, a trend which clearly displays the influence of Takuboku's *seikatsu-ha* sensibility. As long as this verse form remains, Takuboku's name as one of the great pioneers of modern tanka will be remembered by those who find pleasure and comfort in this form of poetry.

English Titles and Subdivision Titles of Takuboku's Works Cited

"After Endless Discussions"   "Hateshinaki Giron no Ato"
"An Afternoon in My Study"   "Shosai no Gogo"
"An Airplane"   "Hikōki"
"The Bell at Twilight"   "Boshō"
The Benign Divine Spirit   *Nigitama*
"A Bunch of Autumn Grass"   "Akikusa Hitotaba"
Clouds Are Geniuses   *Kumo wa Tensai de Aru*
Crimson Medic   *Beni Magoyashi*
"A Criticism of *Young Leaves   "Kusawakaba o Hyōsu"
  of Grass*"
"A Cuckoo"   "Kanko-dori"
"A Dialogue Between an Egoist   "Ichi Rikoshugisha to Yūjin
  and His Friend"   to no Taiwa"
"Don't Wake Up!"   "Okiruna"
Drifting   *Hyōhaku*
"Dysentery"   "Sekiri"
"The Echo"   "Yamabiko"
"The Epitaph"   "Bohimei"
"The Evening Bell"   "Yoru no Kane"
"The Fist"   "Kobushi"
"Footprints"   "Ashiato"
"From Shibutami Village"   "Shibutami-mura yori"
"From Yumi-chō: Poems to Eat"   "Yumi-chō yori: Kuraubeki Shi"
The Funeral Procession   *Sōretsu*
"The Ginko Tree"   "Ichō no Ki"
"The Good Feel of the   "Akikaze no Kokoroyosa ni"
  Autumn Wind"
A Handful of Sand   *Ichiaku no Suna*
"Hasty Ideas"   "Sekkachi na Shisō"
"Heated Argument"   "Gekiron"
"The Hidden Marsh"   "Komorinu"
"The Horror of a Town in   "Natsu no Machi no Kyōfu"
  Summer"

The Hospital Window	*Byōin no Mado*
"A House"	"Ie"
"The Ideas of Richard Wagner"	"Waguneru no Shisō"
"In Memory of Tsunajima Ryōsen"	"Tsunajima Ryōsen-shi o Tomurau"
Japanese Anarchist Conspiracy Incident: Proceedings and Related Phenomena	*Nihon Museifushugisha Inbō-jiken Keika oyobi Futai-genshō*
"A Letter from the Forest"	"Rinchūsho"
"The Literary World of May"	"Gogatsu no Bundan"
A Little World	*Shōtenchi*
Longing	*Akogare*
"Love Songs to Myself"	"Ware o Aisuru Uta"
"The Moon and the Bell"	"Tsuki to Kane"
"Mother"	"Haha"
"Mr. Kikuchi"	"Kikuchi-kun"
"On a Fallen Roof-tile"	"Ochigawara no Fu"
"On Opening a Worn-out Bag"	"Furubitaru Kaban o Akete"
"One Branch on a Table"	"Takujō Isshi"
Our Gang and He	*Warera no Ichidan to Kare*
"The Peaceful Resort"	"Kantenchi"
"A Postcard"	"Hagaki"
Power and Poetry	*Yobiko to Kuchibue*
"The Present State of the Age of Repression: The Fall of Authoritative Power and of Pure Naturalism and the Examination of Tomorrow"	"Jidai Heisoku no Genjō: Kyōken, Junsui Shizenshugi no Saigo oyobi Asu no Kōsatsu"
"The Road"	"Michi"
"Reminiscence of the Forest"	"Mori no Omoide"
The Rōmaji Diary	*Rōmaji Nikki*
Sad Toys	*Kanashiki Gangu*
The Shadow of a Bird	*Chōei*
"The Shadow of a Tower"	"Tōei"
"The Ship of Life"	"Inochi no Fune"
Shizuko's Sorrow	*Shizuko no Kanashimi*
"The Sleeping City"	"Nemureru Miyako"
"Smoke"	"Kemuri"
"The Snowy Evening"	"Yuki no Yo"
"The Solitary House"	"Hitotsu Ie"
"The Song of a Flower Guardian"	"Hanamori no Uta"
"A Spoonful of Cocoa"	"Kokoa no Hito-saji"
"Sporadic Feelings and Reflections"	"Kiregire ni Kokoro ni Ukanda Kanji to Kaisō"

Notes and References

Chapter One

1. Miura Mitsuko, *Ani Takuboku no Omoide (Reminscences of My Brother Takuboku)* (Tokyo: Rironsha, 1964), p. 18.

2. A life-long friend of Takuboku, Kindaichi later distinguished himself as a linguist specializing in the Ainu language. Noted for his translation of the Ainu epic, *Yūkara*, he also authored a book on Takuboku and was one of the editors of the edition of Takuboku's works cited below. The other close friend of Takuboku was Miyazaki Daishirō whom Takuboku met in Hakodate, Hokkaido. See pp. 23–24.

3. Yuza Shōgo, *Takuboku to Shibutami (Takuboku and Shibutami)* (Tokyo: Yaegaki Shobō, 1971), pp. 83ff.

4. Donald Keene, *Landscape and Portraits* (Palo Alto and Tokyo: Kōdansha International, 1971), pp. 134–35. I owe much to Keene's study for the information concerning the development of "the poems in the new style."

5. Keene, p. 136.

6. *Takuboku Zenshū (The Complete Works of Takuboku)*, eds. Kindaichi Kyōsuke and others (Tokyo: Chikuma Shobō, 1967–68), V, 63. All citations from Takuboku's works are from this edition. Hereafter references to volume and page numbers are shown in the text. In April, 1978, Chikuma Shobō began publishing the definitive edition of Takuboku's complete works in eight volumes, to be completed in November, 1978. This edition was not ready in time to be used in the present study.

7. The Naturalist movement in Japan, along with Takuboku's attitudes toward it, will be discussed in detail in Chapter 3.

8. See Richard Storry, *A History of Modern Japan* (London: Penguin Books, 1960), pp. 147–48. Also consult *Ishikawa Takuboku Jiten (Ishikawa Takuboku Handbook)*, ed. Shidai Ryūzō (Tokyo: Meiji Shoin, 1970), pp. 124–26. A discussion of Takuboku's attitude toward the Incident is contained in Yoshida Koyō, *Ishikawa Takuboku to Taigyaku Jiken (Ishikawa Takuboku and the High Treason Incident)* (Tokyo: Meiji Shoin, 1967).

Chapter Two

1. For this point I am indebted to Kuwabara Takeo. See his celebrated essay, "Takuboku no Nikki" ("Takuboku's Diary"), in *Takuboku Zenshū (Takuboku's Works)* (Tokyo: Iwanami Shoten, 1954), XVII, 74.
2. Quoted by Yoshida Seiichi, *Shizenshugi no Kenkyū (A Study of Naturalism)* (Tokyo: Tokyo-dō, 1958), II, 156.
3. Quoted by Iwaki Yukinori, *Ishikawa Takuboku (Collected Works of Ishikawa Takuboku)* (Tokyo: Yūseidō, 1966), p. 314.
4. William Theodore de Bary, ed., *The Buddhist Tradition in India, China and Japan* (New York: Random House, 1969), p. 347.
5. Kunisaki Mokutarō, *Takuboku-ron Josetsu (A Critical Introduction to Takuboku)* (Kyoto: Hōritsu Bunkasha, 1960), pp. 124–25.

Chapter Three

1. All of Takuboku's western style poems can be found in the second volume of *The Complete Works of Takuboku.*
2. See for example an entry in his diary dated November 7, 1902: "Oh, glaring city [Tokyo]! Bewildered by the bustle of the city many have changed into skeletons with no honest hearts. I have seen several pitiful friends who have become just that.

"The dusty storm with ill odor blows into every corner of the city. . ." (V, 13).
3. Kunisaki, p. 221.
4. Iwaki, pp. 332–33.
5. Iwaki, p. 333.
6. Compare Kunisaki's observation:

"This poem is not derived from any concrete experience of daily life; it is the offspring of Takuboku's poetic imagination. In other words, the imagination was not nourished enough by the nutrition of actual experience." See Kunisaki, p. 226.

Chapter Four

1. The manuscript of *Vestige,* written almost simultaneously with *Clouds Are Geniuses,* was burned in the Hakodate fire in the summer of 1907.
2. See Kubokawa Tsurujirō, "Ishikawa Takuboku-ron—Shōsetsu o Chūshin to shite—" ("A Critical Study of Ishikawa Takuboku with Special Emphasis on His Novels"), *Shichō,* 1 (1946).
3. Kubokawa, 97.
4. Kubokawa, 97.
5. Kubokawa, *Ishikawa Takuboku* (Tokyo: Kōbundō, 1970), p. 92.
6. Odagiri Hideo, *Ishikawa Takuboku no Sekai (The World of Ishikawa Takuboku)* (Tokyo: Ushio Shuppan, 1971), p. 124.

Chapter Five

1. See Takuboku's own comment on his change in poetic sensibility, a passage quoted in Chapter 3, p. 86.

2. For these figures I am indebted to Iwaki, *Ishikawa Takuboku (A Biographical Study of Ishikawa Takuboku)* (Tokyo: Yoshikawa Kōbunkan, 1961), pp. 195–98.

3. All quotations of tanka from *A Handful of Sand* and *Sad Toys* are from Volume I of *The Complete Works of Takuboku*.

4. For a valuable study of Takuboku's treatment of his childhood home in his tanka, see Ōkushi Sachiko, "Takuboku ni okeru 'Furusato' Shibo" ("Takuboku's Nostalgia for His Childhood Home"), *Nihon Bungaku*, 15 (February 1966), 140–49; and Yuza, pp. 165–87.

5. Quoted by Iwaki, *Collected Works of Ishikawa Takuboku*, p. 285.

Chapter Six

1. Watanabe Junzō, "Shisaku to Zenshin—Takuboku no Shisō" ("Contemplation and Progress: Takuboku's Ideas"), in *Shinpen Ishikawa Takuboku Senshū (New Selected Works of Ishikawa Takuboku)*, ed. Watanabe Junzō and Ishikawa Masao (Tokyo: Shunjūsha, 1961), VII, 164.

2. Ōhashi Matsuhei, ed., *Gendai Tanka Zenshū (Collections of Modern Tanka)* (Tokyo: Sōgensha, 1952), V, 251.

3. Itō Sei and Yoshida Seiichi, eds., *Akutagawa Ryūnosuke Zenshū (The Complete Works of Akutagawa Ryūnosuke)* (Tokyo: Kadokawa Shoten, 1967–68), IX, 125.

Selected Bibliography

PRIMARY SOURCES

1. Complete Works of Takuboku

KINDAICHI KYŌSUKE and others, eds. *Takuboku Zenshū (The Complete Works of Takuboku)*. 8 vols. Tokyo: Chikuma Shobō, 1967–1968. The most up-to-date edition. Replaces the Iwanami Shoten edition of *Takuboku's Works* (17 vols., 1953–1954), which had been long regarded as the most reliable collection of Takuboku's works. Carefully edited with helpful commentary at the end of each volume. The eighth volume is a collection of essays by Takuboku's friends and leading scholars and critics. Among them are Yosano Tekkan, Miyazaki Ikuu, Kindaichi Kyōsuke, Iwaki Yukinori, Odagiri Hideo, Imai Yasuko and Kunisaki Mokutarō. A comprehensive bibliography and a detailed chronology are provided at the end of Volume 8. In April, 1978, Chikuma Shobō began publishing the definitive edition of Takuboku's complete works in eight volumes, to be completed in November, 1978.

2. Selected Works of Takuboku

In Japanese

ARA MASATO, ed. *Ishikawa Takuboku*. Tokyo: Kawade Shobō Shinsha, 1962. Along with selected works of Takuboku this book includes articles by leading Takuboku critics.

IMAI YASUKO, ed. *Ishikawa Takuboku Shū (Collected Works of Ishikawa Takuboku)*. Tokyo: Kadokawa Shoten, 1969. Carefully annotated edition of Takuboku's works with a helpful introduction by Iwaki Yukinori. All the major works of Takuboku from each genre are included along with an up-to-date bibliography and detailed chronology. A reliable and readily available edition of Takuboku's major works.

IWAKI YUKINORI, ed. *Ishikawa Takuboku (Collected Works of Ishikawa Takuboku)*. Tokyo: Yūseidō, 1966. Fewer works included than in Imai's book cited above, but copiously annotated by the foremost scholar-critic of Takuboku. Annotated bibliography attached. A handy introductory text of Takuboku's life and writings.

195

NAKANO SHIGEHARU and KUBOKAWA TSURUJIRŌ, eds. *Ishikawa Takuboku*. Tokyo: Kadokawa Shoten, 1960. Takuboku's select representative works are chronologically arranged according to the literary movements which influenced his development. The second half is a collection of essays by seven well known critics.

In English

HONDA H. H., trans. *The Poetry of Ishikawa Takuboku*. Tokyo: Hokuseidō Press, 1959. In addition to select representative tanka from *A Handful of Sand* and *Sad Toys*, some tanka written in Takuboku's teens are translated.

KEENE, DONALD, ed. *Modern Japanese Literature*. New York: Grove Press, 1956. Contains eleven tanka translations done by Sakanishi Shio whose work is cited below.

―――, trans. "The Romaji Diary." *Modern Japanese Literature*. New York: Grove Press, 1956. pp. 211–31. An excellent translation of Takuboku's best known diary.

SAKANISHI SHIO, trans. *A Handful of Sand*. Tokyo: Dokusho Tenbōsha, 1947. The first serious attempt at English translation of Takuboku's tanka and poems in the western style. 104 tanka from *A Handful of Sand* and thirty-four from *Sad Toys* along with twelve western style poems are translated into English. Introduction contains a succinct and informative account of Takuboku's development as a tanka poet.

SESAR, CARL, trans. *Takuboku: Poems to Eat*. Palo Alto and Tokyo: Kōdansha International, 1966. Eighty-five tanka from *A Handful of Sand*, fifty-nine from *Sad Toys* and thirty-seven from those published in various magazines are put into English. Thus far the best of all English translations of Takuboku's tanka.

TAKAMINE HIROSHI, trans. *A Sad Toy: Takuboku's Life and Poems*. Tokyo: Tokyo News Service, 1962. An account of Takuboku's life through an examination of tanka from *A Handful of Sand*. Contains interesting observations on Takuboku's use of vowel sounds. Translations of the tanka are interpretative.

SECONDARY SOURCES

In Japanese

A great number of books and articles on Takuboku have been written by close friends and acquaintances as well as scholars and critics. As there are virtually no critical studies available in English, however, the following list includes only a selection of studies in japanese directly related to Takuboku which I have found helpful in writing this book.

ISHIMODA SHŌ. *Zoku Rekishi to Minzoku no Hakken* (*History and Ethnic Identity*, second series). Tokyo: Tokyo Daigaku, 1953. Though not a work of literary criticism, this volume includes a chapter devoted to

Takuboku's ideas and tanka. Takuboku is seen as a serious thinker, critic and poet who attempted to identify himself with the people of his native land.

IWAKI YUKINORI. *Ishikawa Takuboku Hyōden (A Critical Biography of Ishikawa Takuboku)*. Tokyo: Tōhō Shobō, 1955. Definitive biography written with great attention to detail.

_____. *Ishikawa Takuboku (A Biographical Study of Ishikawa Takuboku)*. Tokyo: Yoshikawa Kōbunkan, 1961. A shorter version of the definitive biography. A useful introduction to Takuboku.

KINDAICHI KYOSUKE. *Shintei Ishikawa Takuboku (Ishikawa Takuboku, Revised)*. Tokyo: Kadokawa Shoten, 1955. A memoir by Takuboku's lifelong friend. Conveys vividly the personality of Takuboku the man.

KUBOKAWA TSURUJIRŌ. *Ishikawa Takuboku*. Tokyo: Kōbundō Shobō, 1970. Attempts to show Takuboku's achievement as a novelist, a long neglected area in Takuboku criticism.

KUNISAKI MOKUTARŌ. *Takuboku-ron Josetsu (A Critical Introduction to Takuboku)*. Kyoto: Hōritsu Bunkasha, 1960. An original approach to Takuboku. Attempts to present a total picture of Takuboku through a close examination of each genre he tried. Draws attention to existentialist elements in Takuboku's works.

KUWABARA TAKEO. "Takuboku no Nikki" ("Takuboku's Diary"). *Takuboku Zenshū (Takuboku's Works)*. Tokyo: Iwanami Shoten, 1953–1954. XVII, 64–82.

MIURA MITSUKO. *Ani Takuboku no Omoide (Reminiscences of My Brother Takuboku)*. Tokyo: Rironsha, 1964. A memoir of Takuboku by his younger sister. An informative inside story of Takuboku the man.

MURANO SHIRŌ. "Takuboku no Shi ni tsuite" ("On Takuboku's Western-style Poems"). *Kokubungaku Kaishaku to Kyōzai no Kenkyū*, April 1958, pp. 36–47. Thinks highly of a series of poems in "A Study of the Heart," which he considers full of genuine human emotion.

NAKANO SHIGEHARU. *Takuboku*. Tokyo: Kōbundō, 1951. Includes an influential essay written in 1926, in which he attempted to define Takuboku's place as a socialist critic of Japanese society.

NIHON BUNGAKU KENKYŪ SHIRYŌ ZŌSHO. *Ishikawa Takuboku*. Tokyo: Yūseidō, 1970. Thirty-one essays about Takuboku's ideas, poems, novels and tanka by leading scholars and critics. Among them are Donald Keene, "Takuboku no Nikki to Geijutsu" ("Takuboku's Diary and Artistry"), written in Japanese, which stresses the literary value of Takuboku's diary, particularly of *The Rōmaji Diary*; Imai Yasuko, "Takuboku no Shizenshugi e no Sekkin" ("Takuboku's Attempt at Naturalism"), which analyzes *The Shadow of a Bird* as a carefully planned Naturalistic novel; and Katsura Koji, "Ichiaku no Suna Shiron" ("A Personal View of *A Handful of Sand*"), in which Takuboku's three-line tanka are closely compared and contrasted with those of Toki Aika.

ODAGIRI HIDEO. *Ishikawa Takuboku no Sekai (The World of Ishikawa Takuboku)*. Tokyo: Ushio Shuppan, 1971. Comprised of critical essays originally written for the Chikuma Shobō edition of Takuboku's complete works. A comprehensive study of Takuboku's tanka, western style poems, novels, essays and diary. A reliable and readily available critical study.

OKUSHI SACHIKO. "*Takuboku ni okeru 'Furusato' Shibo*" ("Takuboku's Nostalgia for his Childhood Home"). *Nihon Bungaku*, 15 (February 1966), 140-49. A valuable study of Takuboku's treatment of the image of home in his works.

SHIDAI RYŪZO, ed. *Ishikawa Takuboku Jiten (Ishikawa Takuboku Handbook)*. Tokyo: Meiji Shoin, 1970. A very useful handbook with a glossary of special terms used by Takuboku and a detailed chronology.

SŌMA TSUNEO. "*Rōmaji Nikki ni tsuite—Takuboku Nōto*" ("On *The Rōmaji Diary:* A Note on Takuboku"). *Nihon Bungaku*, 9 (February 1960), 104-15. Interprets this diary as a Naturalistic, confessional I-novel.

SUGIMORI HISAHIDE. *Takuboku no Kanashiki Shōgai (The Sad Life of Takuboku)*. Tokyo: Kadokawa Shoten, 1970. A critical biography of the writer. Attempts to correct the idealized image of Takuboku so as to present a more true to life picture of the man.

SUGIMOTO TSUTOMU. "*Atehamaranu Muyō no Kagi—Ishikawa Takuboku Rōmaji Nikki no Kenkyu*" ("A Key That Does Not Fit: A Study of Takuboku's *The Rōmaji Diary*"). *Gendai Bungaku Josetsu*, 2 (1963), 65-81. Examines the diary in the context of the Meiji interest in modernizing Japanese. Attempts to show that Takuboku used rōmaji in an effort to simplify the complex Japanese writing system.

TAKAKUWA SUMIO. *Nihon no Hyūmanisuto (Japanese Humanists)*. Tokyo: Eihōsha, 1957. Chapter 5 deals with Takuboku. Maintains that Takuboku's works reflect too much self-centeredness to categorize him as a writer genuinely concerned with human problems.

WATANABE JUNZŌ. "*Shisaku to Zenshin—Takuboku no Shisō*" ("Contemplation and Progress: Takuboku's Ideas") *Shinsen Ishikawa Takuboku Senshū (New Selected Works of Ishikawa Takuboku)*. Eds. Watanabe Junzō and Ishikawa Masao. Tokyo: Shunjūsha, 1961. VII, 133-70. A study of Takuboku's development as a thinker with special emphasis on his bent toward socialism at the end of his career.

YOSHIDA KOYŌ. *Ishikawa Takuboku to Taigyaku Jiken (Ishikawa Takuboku and the High Treason Incident)*. Tokyo: Meiji Shoin, 1967. The most comprehensive study of the subject. Carefully examines Takuboku's diary, essays, western style poems and tanka.

YUZA SHŌGO. *Takuboku to Shibutami (Takuboku and Shibutami)*. Tokyo: Yaegaki Shobō, 1971. Along with a new account about Takuboku's cheating at Morioka Middle School, it contains an interesting study of the conception of *furusato* ("childhood home") in Takuboku's works, particularly in his tanka.

In English

KEENE, DONALD. *Landscape and Portraits*. Palo Alto and Tokyo: Kōdansha International, 1971. In the section "Modern Japanese Poetry," pp. 131-56, Takuboku is referred to in relation to the development of modern Japanese poetry in the western style, and in "Shiki and Takuboku," pp. 157-70, Takuboku's life and works are briefly compared and contrasted with those of the foremost innovator of modern haiku, Masaoka Shiki.

Index

107920

DATE DUE

895.61
I79H
1979   107920

AUTHOR

Hijiya, Yukihito

TITLE

Ishikawa Takuboku.

DATE DUE	BORROWER'S NAME	ROOM NUMBER
04 16 5		
04 16 5	RETURNED	

895.61
I79H
1979
Hijiya, Yukihito
Ishikawa Takuboku.

Ohio Dominican College Library
1216 Sunbury Road
Columbus, Ohio 43219

DEMCO